Raspberry Pi Computer Architecture Essentials

Explore Raspberry Pi's architecture through innovative and fun projects

Andrew K. Dennis

PUBLISHING

BIRMINGHAM - MUMBAI

Raspberry Pi Computer Architecture Essentials

First published: March 2016

Production reference: 1170316

Published by Packt Publishing Ltd.
Livery Place
35 Livery Street
Birmingham B3 2PB, UK.

ISBN 978-1-78439-797-5

www.packtpub.com

Credits

Author
Andrew K. Dennis

Reviewer
Ed Snajder

Commissioning Editor
Amarabha Banerjee

Acquisition Editor
Divya Poojari

Content Development Editor
Trusha Shriyan

Technical Editor
Shivani Kiran Mistry

Copy Editor
Safis Editing

Project Coordinator
Kinjal Bari

Proofreader
Safis Editing

Indexer
Rekha Nair

Production Coordinator
Melwyn Dsa

Cover Work
Melwyn Dsa

About the Author

Andrew K. Dennis is the manager of professional services software development at Prometheus Research. Prometheus Research is a leading provider of integrated data management for research and is the home of HTSQL, an open source navigational query language for RDBMS.

Andrew has a diploma in computing, a BSc in software engineering, and is currently studying for a second BSc in creative computing in his spare time.

He has over 12 years of experience working in the software industry in the UK, Canada, and the USA. This experience includes e-learning courseware development, custom CMS and LMS development, SCORM consultancy, web development in a variety of languages, open source application development, blogging about the integration of web technologies with electronics for home automation, and punching lots of Cat5 cables.

His interests include web development, e-learning, 3D printing, Linux, the Raspberry Pi and Arduino, open source projects, home automation and the use of web technology in this sphere, amateur electronics, home networking, and software engineering.

About the Reviewer

Ed Snajder is a database engineer and hardware hacker working at Jive Software. When not breaking databases and distributed data systems, Ed spends a lot of time in the community evangelizing Raspberry Pi, Arduino, and open source 3D printing. His belief is that if every child could have a Raspberry Pi, we will soon have the flying cars we've always dreamed of. He lives in Portland, Oregon, with his partner, Lindsay and his Shih-Tzus, Obi-wan and Gizmo.

www.PacktPub.com

eBooks, discount offers, and more

Did you know that Packt offers eBook versions of every book published, with PDF and ePub files available? You can upgrade to the eBook version at www.PacktPub.com and as a print book customer, you are entitled to a discount on the eBook copy. Get in touch with us at customercare@packtpub.com for more details.

At www.PacktPub.com, you can also read a collection of free technical articles, sign up for a range of free newsletters and receive exclusive discounts and offers on Packt books and eBooks.

https://www2.packtpub.com/books/subscription/packtlib

Do you need instant solutions to your IT questions? PacktLib is Packt's online digital book library. Here, you can search, access, and read Packt's entire library of books.

Why subscribe?

- Fully searchable across every book published by Packt
- Copy and paste, print, and bookmark content
- On demand and accessible via a web browser

Table of Contents

Preface

Are you interested in the myriad features of your Raspberry Pi 2? From the hardware to the software, do you wish to understand how you can interact with these features?

Then this is the book for you!

The Raspberry Pi 2 is one of the latest hardware offerings in the Raspberry Pi family. With many new and improved features than previous versions, there is so much more an enthusiast can do.

This book will walk you through how you can get the most out of your device.

You will learn about how to program on the Raspberry Pi using the Assembly language, Python, and C/C++. This will include building a web server in Python and saving data to an SQLite database. Ever wondered what threads are? These are covered here too.

In addition to this, you will explore the various types of GPIO pins and how these can be used to interact with third party microcontrollers and electronic circuits.

The sound and graphics capabilities of the Raspberry Pi 2 are also experimented with through a number of projects. And to expand the Raspberry Pi's storage option, we will also set up an external HDD via USB.

Finally, the book concludes with a project that brings together many of the technologies explained throughout the chapters.

By the time you finish reading this book, you'll have a firm knowledge of the Raspberry Pi 2 and how you can devise your own projects that use its capabilities.

What this book covers

Chapter 1, Introduction to the Raspberry Pi's Architecture and Setup, provides an introduction to the Raspberry Pi and its hardware architecture. We will explore the various hardware components in detail, and this will provide a basis for the programming projects in future chapters. A quick guide to getting Raspbian installed and SSH enabled is also provided.

Chapter 2, Programming on Raspbian, provides an introduction to the programming languages used in this book. An explanation will be provided of which language is used and why. This chapter will also guide you through setting up the tools for Assembler, C/C++, and Python. Three introduction programs will then be walked through to give you the opportunity to test that your setup works.

Chapter 3, Low-Level Development with Assembly Language, explores programming in the Raspbian operating system using the Assembler programming language.

Chapter 4, Multithreaded Applications with C/C++, having looked at Assembler, we move up the programming hierarchy to C/C++. We learn how to write multithreaded applications and understand their usefulness. Through these applications, we learn more about the multi-core CPU of the Raspberry Pi 2.

Chapter 5, Expanding on Storage Options, offers a guide to expanding the storage options of the Raspberry Pi beyond the SD card.

Chapter 6, Low-Level Graphics Programming, shows you how to interact with the graphics hardware on the Raspberry Pi 2. Here you will learn how to draw to the screen via the frame buffer.

Chapter 7, Exploring the Raspberry Pi's GPIO Pins, shows you how to interact with electronic components using the Raspberry PI's GPIO pins. Here we look at how Python libraries can be used to simplify the process.

Chapter 8, Exploring Sound with the Raspberry Pi 2, gives an introduction to the basics of sound programming using the Raspberry Pi's hardware. Learn about live coding via the Sonic-Pi IDE to generate your own algorithmic music.

Chapter 9, Building a Web Server, expands upon your knowledge of Python to build a web server via Flask. This chapter explores the Ethernet and Wi-Fi capabilities of the Raspberry Pi for delivering web-based applications. In this chapter, you will also learn about using SQLite to store data and display it via a web page. Topics covered also include Apache and NGINX.

Chapter 10, Integrating with Third-Party Microcontrollers, in this chapter we learn how to interact with third-party microcontrollers such as the Arduino. These devices can form the basis of robotics projects and augment the abilities of the Raspberry Pi.

Chapter 11, Final Project, will conclude the book with a final project that brings together many of the topics explored throughout previous chapters.

What you need for this book

The following list provides an overview of the recommended and optional hardware needed for the projects in this book. Where hardware is needed for a specific chapter, the relevant chapter is listed:

- Raspberry Pi 2.
- USB keyboard.
- HDMI monitor.
- USB mouse.
- MicroSD card.
- Wall power unit for the Raspberry Pi 2.
- A working Internet connection.
- A selection of wires for connecting to the GPIO pins; 12 recommended for *Chapter 7, Exploring the Raspberry Pi's GPIO pins, Chapter 10, Integrating with Third-Party Microcontrollers,* and *Chapter 11, Final Project.*
- An LED for *Chapter 7, Exploring the Raspberry Pi's GPIO pins* and *Chapter 11, Final Project.*
- 1.6K, 3.3k Ohm resistor for *Chapter 10, Integrating with Third-Party Microcontrollers.*
- 270 Ohm resistor for *Chapter 7, Exploring the Raspberry Pi's GPIO pins* and *Chapter 11, Final Project.*
- USB hard drive for *Chapter 5, Expanding on Storage Options.*
- Cooking Hacks Raspberry Pi to Arduino Bridge Shield or Pi Cobbler. These are optional and not necessary, as the breadboard can replace these.
- Breadboard. Only required if not using a third-party shield. Needed for *Chapter 7, Exploring the Raspberry Pi's GPIO pins, Chapter 10, Integrating with Third-Party Microcontrollers,* and *Chapter 11, Final Project.*
- Arduino Uno. Needed for *Chapter 10, Integrating with Third-Party Microcontrollers.*
- USB cable to connect Arduino to Raspberry Pi. Needed for *Chapter 10, Integrating with Third-Party Microcontrollers.*

Who this book is for

Are you interested in the architecture that forms the Raspberry Pi 2? Would you like to learn how its components work through interactive projects?

This book provides a hands-on guide to the Raspberry Pi 2's hardware and software. Each chapter builds upon the last to develop applications and electronics that leverage many of the features of the Raspberry Pi 2. From programming sound to integrating with third party microcontrollers, it's all covered here.

Aimed at the Raspberry Pi enthusiast, this is a perfect introductory text on how to get the most out of your new device.

While understanding programming concepts is helpful, no prior knowledge of the programming languages covered in this book is required.

Some simple electronics projects are included but no soldering is required.

Conventions

In this book, you will find a number of text styles that distinguish between different kinds of information. Here are some examples of these styles and an explanation of their meaning.

Code words in text, database table names, folder names, filenames, file extensions, pathnames, dummy URLs, user input, and Twitter handles are shown as follows: "The cd command allows you to change directories."

A block of code is set as follows:

```
int main(void)
{
int a;
printf("Please input an integer: ");
scanf("%d", &a);
printf("You entered the number: %d\n", a);
return 0;
}
```

Any command-line input or output is written as follows:

```
mv /home/pi/test.txt /home/pi/test2.txt
```

New terms and **important words** are shown in bold. Words that you see on the screen, for example, in menus or dialog boxes, appear in the text like this: "Click on the **Generate** button."

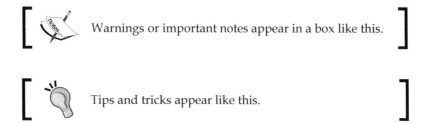

Warnings or important notes appear in a box like this.

Tips and tricks appear like this.

Reader feedback

Feedback from our readers is always welcome. Let us know what you think about this book—what you liked or disliked. Reader feedback is important for us as it helps us develop titles that you will really get the most out of.

To send us general feedback, simply e-mail feedback@packtpub.com, and mention the book's title in the subject of your message.

If there is a topic that you have expertise in and you are interested in either writing or contributing to a book, see our author guide at www.packtpub.com/authors.

Customer support

Now that you are the proud owner of a Packt book, we have a number of things to help you to get the most from your purchase.

Downloading the example code

You can download the example code files for this book from your account at http://www.packtpub.com. If you purchased this book elsewhere, you can visit http://www.packtpub.com/support and register to have the files e-mailed directly to you.

You can download the code files by following these steps:

1. Log in or register to our website using your e-mail address and password.
2. Hover the mouse pointer on the **SUPPORT** tab at the top.
3. Click on **Code Downloads & Errata**.
4. Enter the name of the book in the **Search** box.
5. Select the book for which you're looking to download the code files.
6. Choose from the drop-down menu where you purchased this book from.
7. Click on **Code Download**.

Once the file is downloaded, please make sure that you unzip or extract the folder using the latest version of:

- WinRAR / 7-Zip for Windows
- Zipeg / iZip / UnRarX for Mac
- 7-Zip / PeaZip for Linux

Errata

Although we have taken every care to ensure the accuracy of our content, mistakes do happen. If you find a mistake in one of our books—maybe a mistake in the text or the code—we would be grateful if you could report this to us. By doing so, you can save other readers from frustration and help us improve subsequent versions of this book. If you find any errata, please report them by visiting http://www.packtpub.com/submit-errata, selecting your book, clicking on the **Errata Submission Form** link, and entering the details of your errata. Once your errata are verified, your submission will be accepted and the errata will be uploaded to our website or added to any list of existing errata under the Errata section of that title.

To view the previously submitted errata, go to https://www.packtpub.com/books/content/support and enter the name of the book in the search field. The required information will appear under the **Errata** section.

Piracy

Piracy of copyrighted material on the Internet is an ongoing problem across all media. At Packt, we take the protection of our copyright and licenses very seriously. If you come across any illegal copies of our works in any form on the Internet, please provide us with the location address or website name immediately so that we can pursue a remedy.

Please contact us at copyright@packtpub.com with a link to the suspected pirated material.

We appreciate your help in protecting our authors and our ability to bring you valuable content.

Questions

If you have a problem with any aspect of this book, you can contact us at questions@packtpub.com, and we will do our best to address the problem.

1

Introduction to the Raspberry Pi's Architecture and Setup

This chapter provides a brief introduction to the Raspberry Pi 2 Model B including both its history and its hardware architecture.

As well as discussing its system architecture, we will also look at some time saving methods for installing the Raspbian operating system.

Finally, we will wrap up with a number of tips and tricks, including how to monitor the voltage, overclock the CPU, and check the device's temperature. These quick tips should get you started exploring the operating system, installing software, and investigating the hardware.

We will mainly focus on the following topics:

- Raspberry Pi hardware architecture and components
- Installing Raspbian via a boot loader and enabling and testing SSH with RSA keys

History and background of the Raspberry Pi

The Raspberry Pi is a credit card-sized computer designed and manufactured in the UK with the initial intention of providing a cheap computing device for education. Since its release, however, it has grown far beyond the sphere of academia.

Its origins can be found in the University of Cambridge's Computer Laboratory in 2006. Computer scientist Eben Upton, along with Rob Mullins, Jack Lang and Alan Mycroft, were concerned that incoming computing undergraduate students had grown divorced from the technical aspects of computing. This was largely due to school syllabuses that placed an emphasis on using computers rather than understanding them.

Off the back of this initial concern, the Raspberry Pi foundation was formed. Over the next six years the team worked on developing a cheap and accessible device that would help schools to teach concepts such as programming, thus bringing students closer to understanding how computing works.

The Raspberry Pi's initial commercial release was in February 2012. Since then, the board has gone through a number of revisions and has been available in two models, those being Model A and Model B.

The Model A device is the cheaper and simpler of the two computers and the Model B the more powerful, including support for Ethernet connectivity.

In February 2015, the Raspberry Pi 2 Model B was released, and this is the device discussed in this book.

The new Raspberry Pi 2 is significantly more powerful than previous versions, opening us up to many new possibilities.

We will now look at the hardware of the device to get a basic understanding of what it is capable of doing. Future chapters will build upon the basics presented here.

Raspberry Pi hardware specifications

The new Raspberry Pi is built on the back of the Broadcom BCM2836. The BCM2836 is a system-on-a-chip processor containing four ARM cores and Broadcom's VideoCore® IV graphics stack.

In contrast to this, previous Raspberry Pi A and B models only contained a single core.

On top of this, several other components make up the device, including USB, RCA, and microSD card storage. The previous Raspberry Pi Model B only contained two USB drives and a microUSB compared to the four USB drives and microUSB of the second version.

You can read a good breakdown of how the two boards standup to each other by visiting the following website: `http://www.alphr.com/raspberry-pi-2/1000353/` `raspberry-pi-2-vs-raspberry-pi-b-a-raspberry-pi-comparison`.

So, compared to earlier models, version 2 is a far more capable computer, yet still remains at the same price. The added benefit of having multiple cores allows us to explore different programming techniques for utilizing them.

Next, we shall cover the core components of the Raspberry Pi board in more detail. The following is an image of the board with a description of each component:

Image courtesy of Wikipedia

Dimensions

The Raspberry Pi 2 is a small machine measuring only 85.60 mm x 56 mm x 21 mm and weighing approximately 45g. This small size makes it suitable for embedded projects, home automation devices, arcade machines, or building small multi-device clusters.

System on Chip

The **System on Chip** (**SoC**) architecture that the Raspberry Pi 2 implements is the Broadcom BCM2836, which we touched upon earlier in this chapter. This contains a CPU, GPU, SDRAM, and single USB port. Each of these items is discussed in more detail under the appropriate heading.

CPU

A central processing unit is the brain of your Raspberry Pi. It is responsible for processing machine instructions, which are the result of your compiled programs.

The BCM2836 implements a 900 MHz quad-core ARM Cortex-A7 processor. This runs on the ARMv7 instruction set.

The ARM architecture reference manual can be downloaded from ARM's website at `http://infocenter.arm.com/help/topic/com.arm.doc.ddi0406c/index.html`.

GPU

The graphics processing unit (GPU) is a specialist chip designed to handle the complex mathematics required to render graphics.

The Broadcom VideoCore Iv 250 MHz supports OpenGL ES 2.0 (24 GFLOPS) Mpeg-2 and VC-1 (with license). It also includes a 1080p30 H.264/MPEG-4 AVC decoded/encoder.

The documentation for the GPU can be found on Broadcom's website at `https://www.broadcom.com/docs/support/videocore/VideoCoreIV-AG100-R.pdf`.

SDRAM

The Raspberry Pi 2 comes equipped with 1 GB of SDRAM, which is shared between the GPU and CPU.

4 USB 2.0 ports and 1 SoC on-board USB

The previous version of the Raspberry Pi Model B contained only a single microUSB port and a two standard USB ports. The Raspberry Pi 2 has been expanded to include an onboard 5-port USB hub.

This allows you to connect four standard USB cables to the device and a single microUSB cable. The micro USB port can be used to power your Raspberry Pi 2.

MicroSD card port

The microSD card is the main boot and storage mechanism of the Raspberry Pi. It is upon the microSD card that you will load your operating system and store data. Later in this book we will look at using the microSD purely for booting the Raspberry Pi, and then using a USB hard drive as a storage mechanism. In this chapter, we will delve into how we can setup the SD card with the Raspbian operating system.

Ethernet port

One of the benefits of the Raspberry Pi 2 Model B is that it contains an Ethernet port. Many Raspberry Pi packages available on Amazon and similar stores include a wireless USB dongle; however, this results in you having to use up a USB port. If you plan to place your Raspberry Pi near a router or switch or have enough Ethernet cable, then you can connect your Raspberry Pi directly with the Ethernet jack.

The Raspberry Pi 2 supports 10/100 Mbps Ethernet, and the USB adapter in the third/fourth port of USB hub can also be used for Ethernet via a USB to Ethernet adapter.

Ethernet to USB adapters can be purchased from most good electronics stores and you can read more about the technology at `https://en.wikipedia.org/wiki/Ethernet_over_USB`.

Audio

The Raspberry Pi 2 implements the **Inter-IC Sound (I2S)** serial bus for audio input and output. This allows the device to connect multiple digital audio devices together. A 3.5mm TRRS jack is available and shared with the analog video output. The HDMI component also provides digital audio output.

Further information on configuring the audio output of the Raspberry Pi can be found on the official Raspberry Pi website: `https://www.raspberrypi.org/documentation/configuration/audio-config.md`.

GPIO pins

The main method for interacting with electronic components and expansion boards is through the **general purpose input/output (GPIO)** pins on the Raspberry Pi.

The Raspberry Pi 2 Model B contains 40 pins in total. Future chapters will also look at how we can program these to control electronic devices.

As the acronym suggests the GPIO pins can accept both input and output commands and can be controlled by programs in a variety of languages running on the Raspberry Pi.

The input for example could be readings from a temperature sensor, and the output a command to another device to switch an LED on or off.

The Raspberry *Pinout* project provides an interactive guide to each GPIO pin and can be found at `http://pinout.xyz/`.

Video – analog TV out

As well as providing a digital method for hooking up to a TV or monitor, the Raspberry Pi 2 also comes with analog support. The method of connection is commonly known as a composite or RCA port and earlier models of the Raspberry Pi came specifically with an RCA jack. RCA cables typically come with three connectors, two for audio and one (often yellow) for video.

With the release of the Raspberry Pi 2 the composite video (RCA) and 3.5 mm audio jacks functionality has been merged into a single TRRS hardware component. Therefore, if you wish to use video through this port, you may need to get a 3.5mm Mini AV TRRS to RCA cable instead. These can be found at any good electronics stores or on Amazon.

The Raspberry Pi 2 supports both PAL and NTSC standards.

Video – HDMI port

Also included is a High-Definition Multimedia Interface (HDMI) port. This allows the Raspberry Pi 2 to be hooked up to high definition devices such as televisions and monitors. This port provides a digital alternative to the TRRS jack.

The HDMI port is ideal for streaming video and audio to your TV or monitor.

Basic hardware needed

In order to get up and running with your Raspberry Pi 2 you will need the following additional hardware components:

- MicroSD card
- Micro USB power cable
- Monitor—preferably HDMI
- HDMI cable or 3.5mm to RCA AV cable
- USB keyboard
- USB mouse
- Protective case—optional
- Wi-Fi dongle or Ethernet cable

Many websites offer starter kits that include some of these components, and an existing monitor can be reused.

The eLinux website also provides a good guide to peripherals at `http://elinux.org/RPi_VerifiedPeripherals`.

Before we can power up and start using our Raspberry Pi, however, we need to install an operating system on a microSD card.

The microSD card – the main storage and boot device of the Raspberry Pi 2

A micro secure digital (microSD) card is a portable high performance storage medium used in a variety of electronic devices including cameras, phones and computers. You may already be familiar with them if you use one of the devices we have just listed.

Our Raspberry Pi 2 comes equipped with a microSD slot, which lets us use a microSD card as our main storage and boot mechanism. The card is therefore used in a similar manner to a hard drive on a traditional computer or portable device.

The previous Raspberry Pi models used a standard SD card, which was much larger. Therefore, the microSD card saves space on the circuit board and does not *poke* out as far, reducing the risk of it being broken.

When choosing a microSD card for your projects, there are a variety of brands on the market, and they come in a range of storage sizes running into the tens of gigabytes.

For the projects in this book we recommend using a card with a large amount of storage and you should look at choosing a card that is at *least* 8 GB in size. The NOOBS application, for example, requires a card of at least this size.

The official Raspberry Pi website provides a guide to microSD cards at `http://www.raspberrypi.org/documentation/installation/sd-cards.md` and is a good place to start.

We will now discuss the option of purchasing a microSD card preinstalled with the Raspbian operating system or **New Out Of the Box Software**(**NOOBS**) versus formatting and installing the operating system ourselves.

For those who really wish to understand the Raspberry Pi 2 in detail, installing the operating system from scratch may be a more rewarding experience.

Preinstalled microSD card versus creating your own

A number of websites offer microSD cards preloaded with one of the operating systems that are available for the Raspberry Pi 2. An example can be found at the Allied Electronics website at `http://www.alliedelec.com/raspberry-pi-8gb-sd-card-raspberry-pi-noobs-1-4/70470344/`.

These are a good solution for anybody looking to get up and running quickly or who are not comfortable installing an operating system by themselves from scratch. They are also useful for those who do not have second computer to work with in order to format a new microSD card.

The official Raspberry Pi distributions Element 14 also offer a preinstalled microSD card equipped with NOOBS, a Raspberry Pi 2 operating system boot loader. It can be found at `https://www.element14.com/community/community/raspberry-pi`.

The second option is to purchase a new blank microSD card and follow the instructions contained in this chapter.

It should be noted that if you do not have a home Mac or PC accessible to format a new blank microSD card, then we would recommend acquiring a preformatted card. This should come loaded with either Debian Jessie Raspbian, or the NOOBS boot loader application.

The NOOBS operating system installation manager

This book assumes that the reader will be installing the Raspbian operating system himself or herself. The simplest method for doing this is to install the NOOBS operating system installation manager onto your microSD card.

NOOBS makes the setup of your Raspberry Pi 2 easy and also provides you with a mechanism for choosing other operating systems that are compatible with the Raspberry Pi.

The official Raspberry Pi website contains an introduction and guide to NOOBS and can be found at `http://www.raspberrypi.org/help/noobs-setup/`.

If you already have a blank microSD card, you can download NOOBS from `https://www.raspberrypi.org/downloads/noobs/`.

When installing Raspbian for the first time via NOOBS you will also be presented with the raspi-config screen. This provides some handy shortcuts that allow you to do the following:

- Expand the file system
- Change the user password
- Enable boot to desktop
- Change language
- Enable the camera if you have purchased the peripheral
- Add to Rastrack Raspberry Pi Map
- Overclock your Raspberry Pi
- Explore some advanced configuration options

If you choose not to install Raspbian via NOOBS, then the following section will guide you through the process. If you are using NOOBS you can skip to the *Raspbian installation wrap-up* section.

Downloading the latest version of Raspbian

Your first task will be to download the Raspbian operating system from the official Raspberry Pi website at `https://www.raspberrypi.org/downloads/raspbian/`.

There are several options for downloading Raspbian including an older version of the OS based on Debian Wheezy. We recommend grabbing the latest version, and it can be obtained over either BitTorrent or via a ZIP file.

 The latest version as of September 2015 is Raspbian Jessie

Once you have obtained a copy of the operating system you can move onto formatting your microSD card and installing the image.

Setting up your microSD card and installing the Raspbian operating system

The Raspbian installation process involves two steps:

- Formatting the microSD card to the FAT file system
- Copying the Raspbian image to the card

It is important that we quickly look at what **File Allocation Table (FAT)** is and why we need it.

FAT is a method for defining which sectors of a disk or microSD card files are stored in and which sectors on the disk are free to have new data written to them.

The standard has its origins in the 1970s for use on floppy disks and was developed by Bill Gates and Marc McDonald.

You can read more about FAT here: `https://en.wikipedia.org/wiki/File_Allocation_Table`.

Due to its simplicity of implementation and robustness, this standard is still used on SD and microSD cards today. Therefore, it is the format you will need in order to install the Raspberry Pi's operating system onto your microSD card.

Due to its widespread adoption you may find and microSD card you purchase is already formatted to FAT.

We recommend, however, formatting any new cards you purchase to ensure you do not encounter any problems.

The official Raspberry Pi website provides handy how-to guides for the three major operating systems on how to format and install the Raspbian image.

You can read an up-to-date overview of the installation procedure at `https://www.raspberrypi.org/documentation/installation/installing-images/README.md`.

The following are guides to formatting an SD card for your particular operating system:

- Windows (`https://www.raspberrypi.org/documentation/installation/installing-images/windows.md`)
- Mac OS X (`https://www.raspberrypi.org/documentation/installation/installing-images/mac.md`)
- Linux (`https://www.raspberrypi.org/documentation/installation/installing-images/linux.md`)

Having completed installing the operating system we can now look at some final configuration before exploring some interesting features of Raspbian.

Raspbian installation wrap-up

The following section assumes you have your Raspberry Pi connected to a monitor and with a keyboard and mouse available. It also assumes you have your configuration set to boot to desktop and have powered up and logged into your device.

You should at this point connect your device to your home router. If you are planning on using Wi-Fi, read on.

Now that you have successfully installed Raspbian you should see the Linux desktop.

 If you do not see the desktop, but the command line instead, you can type `startx` to start the GUI.

This desktop contains icons in the top menu linking to a number of programs installed by default with the operating system.

One important icon is the link to **LXTerminal**. This icon launches the Linux terminal window. Click on this icon and you should see the command line load.

The following tasks in this section can all be performed in this window.

As a handy shortcut you can also load the `raspi-config` application at any time by typing the following command:

`sudo raspi-config`

 You can read about the `sudo` command here: `https://www.sudo.ws/`.

If you update settings in this manner you may need to reboot the Raspberry Pi for them to take affect.

Check SSH is running

In order to connect to our Raspberry Pi 2 from another device via a terminal window we need to ensure that the **Secure Shell(SSH)** server is up and running. SSH is the default mechanism for secure communication between our Linux machines. If you used NOOBS to install the OS you may have configured the SSH server at this point via the advanced options. We can check that the SSH service is running successfully as follows.

Open up a terminal window from the Raspbian desktop and type the following command:

```
ps aux | grep sshd
```

The following `sshd` process should be displayed. This tells us the services are up and running:

```
root     2017  0.0  0.3   6228  2892 ?        Ss   15:13   0:00 /usr/sbin/
sshd
```

If the SSH process does not appear, it is simple to start it. Enter the following command into the terminal:

```
sudo /etc/init.d/ssh start
```

After you have executed this command try running the following again and check that the `sshd` process is now running:

```
ps aux | grep sshd
```

By default, to login to the Raspberry Pi 2 over SSH you will be prompted for a username and password. If you have not changed this the username is `pi` and the password is `raspberry`.

In addition to the username and password method, we can also use an RSA key to authenticate and gain access to the Raspberry Pi over a network. We discuss this process next.

RSA key generation for SSH

RSA keys are a useful method to login to the Raspberry Pi. They remove the need to enter a username and password and lock down access to a handful of hardware devices.

A RSA key consists of two parts: a public and private key. A public key can be shared with anyone and any machine with that key on and can in theory let you have access. Therefore, if you purchase more Raspberry Pis, you can place your public key on each, and negate the need to remember multiple passwords.

The private key portion should be kept secret and is located on the machine you will use to access your Raspberry Pi from. For security reasons it is best to keep the private key on a single device.

You can read more about RSA keys and the cryptographic theory behind them here: https://en.wikipedia.org/wiki/RSA_(cryptosystem).

One important piece of information you will need is the IP address or hostname of your Raspberry Pi.

> If Wi-Fi is disabled/not connected, you can enable it via the **Menu | Preferences | WiFi Configuration** link on the desktop

You can obtain this by looking at your local home router, or by running the following commands in the terminal window of Raspbian.

For the IP address, run this command:

```
sudo ip addr show
```

Where to look depends on whether you are using a wireless or wired connection. Ethernet can be found usually at eth0 and wireless at wlan0.

If you would prefer to see the hostname you can run this command:

```
sudo hostname
```

Make a note of this information, as you will need it to connect to the Raspberry Pi 2 from your second device.

If you are using a Mac or Linux to SSH into the Raspberry Pi you can generate the RSA key via the terminal window using the following steps. If you are using Windows, skip to the relevant section further on in this chapter.

Linux and Mac RSA key generation

Start by opening up your Mac or Linux terminal. From the command line run the following command:

```
ssh-keygen -t rsa -b 4096 -C "username"
```

You should replace the username with your own. A message similar to the following will be displayed:

```
Generating public/private rsa key pair.
```

Following this you will see a prompt:

```
Enter file in which to save the key (/Users/username/.ssh/id_rsa):
```

You can press enter here and the key will be saved to the path listed in the prompt. Note that it may look slightly different to the preceding example depending on your username and operating system.

Following this, you have the option of adding a password to the RSA private key. These prevent unauthorized users of your second computer from accessing the Raspberry Pi.

```
Enter passphrase (empty for no passphrase):
Enter same passphrase again:
```

Once you have added a passphrase, the key generation process is complete. You should now see your key's fingerprint:

```
Your identification has been saved in /Users/username/.ssh/id_rsa.
Your public key has been saved in /Users/username/.ssh/id_rsa.pub.
The key fingerprint is:
```

Now we have our key, we need to load it into ssh-agent and then copy it onto the Raspberry Pi 2.

Adding the key to the agent can be done with the following command:

```
ssh-add ~/.ssh/id_rsa
```

This now allows the SSH command to use your key when trying to authenticate.

 If your ssh-agent isn't running, you can use the following command to start it:
```
eval "$(ssh-agent -s)"
```

Before we can SSH into the Raspberry Pi we need to add the public key you created to it.

Thankfully, we can do this in a single command using the Raspberry Pi's default username and password, or if you changed it, that username and password. Run the following command from your terminal. Remember to swap the IP address in the command below with the IP address or hostname you recorded earlier:

```
cat ~/.ssh/id_rsa.pub | ssh user@ip'cat >> .ssh/authorized_keys'
```

With the public key now located on the Raspberry Pi you can attempt to SSH in.

If the .ssh directory and authorized_keys file do not exist on your Raspberry Pi you can create them under the pi user. To create the directory type mkdir .ssh and to create an empty file in this directory type touch authorized_keys.

This can be achieved using the SSH command along with your username and IP address:

```
ssh -A username@ip
```

You will notice that you can now login to the computer remotely and will be presented with a terminal window prompt.

Windows RSA key generation

In order to connect to the Raspberry Pi from a Windows device you will need three pieces of software, Pageant, PuTTY, and PuTTYgen.

Start by downloading PuTTYgen from the following URL: `http://the.earth.li/~sgtatham/putty/latest/x86/puttygen.exe`.

Next download PuTTY from this URL: `http://the.earth.li/~sgtatham/putty/latest/x86/putty.exe`. Like PuTTYgen, this is also an executable you can run from your desktop.

Then finally grab Pageant from this URL: `http://the.earth.li/~sgtatham/putty/latest/x86/pageant.exe`.

We will start by generating our public and private key pair. Open up the PuTTYgen executable.

Once you have this open, run through the following steps:

1. Set the key type as **SSh-2 RSA**.
2. Click on the **Generate** button.
3. You'll now be asked to move your mouse around to generate some random data.
4. Give your key a passphrase.
5. Next, use the **Save private key** button to save the generated private key.
6. Finally, click the **Save public key** button.

Our next task is going to be to add the key to the Raspberry Pi 2's `authorized_keys` file.

 You will need the Raspberry Pi's login details and IP for the next steps.

Open up the PuTTY executable.

From the **Category** list on the left, select **Session** if this is not already open. Now add the following details:

1. In the **Host Name** field, enter the Raspberry Pi's IP address.
2. Set the **Port** to 22.
3. Select the **SSH** radio button.
4. You can now optionally save these details for future connections.
5. Click the **Open** button.

If this is your first connection, you should now see a popup appear called **PuTTY Security Alert**. Click the **Yes** button to move on.

If you entered the connection details successfully, the PuTTY terminal window will now present you with a login prompt for the Raspberry Pi.

You will need to enter in the login name here. By default, this is set as pi; however, you may have changed it if you setup the device via NOOBS.

Following this you will be prompted for the password. This will be raspberry by default, or whichever password you set if you configured Raspbian via NOOBS.

If your login was successful, you should now see the Raspbian command line prompt.

We now want to edit the authorized_key file. We can use the default text editor installed by Raspbian to edit this file. If the file does not exist, you can create it and the .ssh directory.

It is located under the pi user account:

`.ssh/authorized_keys'`

Copy and paste the public key you saved from PuTTYgen into this file.

Save the file and exit it.

You can now logout of the Raspberry Pi.

The final tool we need to test is the Pageant application. This is our windows SSH authentication agent.

Open up the Pageant application. It should be available in the system tray in Windows.

Next, follow these steps:

1. Right click on the **Pageant** icon.
2. Select **Add Key** from the menu.
3. A pop-up will display listing any keys you have.
4. Select the **Add Key** button.
5. From the pop-up window, select the private key you generated with PuTTYgen.
6. Click the **Open** button.
7. Next, you should be prompted to enter the passphrase for your key.
8. Fill this in and click **OK**.
9. You should now see it listed in the **Pageant Key List** window.
10. You can now close the key list.

Whenever you try and access the Raspberry Pi via PuTTY, all you have to enter is the username and host.

Open up PuTTY and connect to the Raspberry Pi again. You should now see you are logged in without a password prompt appearing. This is because you have authenticated your private key against your public key, which was added to the `authorized_keys` list.

 On the first time logging in over SSH you may see a security alert/prompt. You can select **Yes** to this.

This completes setting up access to the Raspberry Pi remotely. We can now add a static IP address and run some diagnostic tests on our device.

We shall now move onto running some tests on the Raspberry Pi via Raspbian. These can be performed either directly on the Pi via the terminal window, or over the SSH connection you just created.

Assign a static IP to your Raspberry Pi 2

Assigning a static IP address to your Raspberry Pi means that when you switch it on or off a new IP will not be assigned. Instead, it will always contain the same IP address, meaning you do not have to hunt down the value assigned to it by the DHCP server each time you reboot.

To start with, check the IP address range on your router and find a free IP address. You will also need the **subnet mask** and the **default gateway**.

Next, we need to assign the free address to the Raspberry Pi. Editing the `interfaces` file can do this:

```
sudo nano /etc/network/interfaces
```

In the open file you will need to locate the line that specifies `eth0` or `wlan0` depending on whether you are wired or wireless. For example:

```
iface eth0 inet dhcp
```

Change the value `dhcp` to static:

```
iface eth0 inet static
```

Once this is done we need to add three lines directly below it specifying the IP address we wish to assign, `netmask`, and `gateway`. You should have these values from checking your router earlier.

 You can always check the `gateway` and `netmask` address directly on the Raspberry Pi by typing: `netstat -rn`.

Paste these in below the interface. An example is show here:

```
address 192.168.1.132
netmask 255.255.255.0
gateway 192.168.1.1
```

Save the file using *Ctrl + X* and press *Y* to save.

We do not need to reboot the Raspberry Pi to apply these changes, but can stop and start the network interface using the following commands:

```
sudo /etc/init.d/networking stop
sudo /etc/init.d/networking start
```

If you now run the command from earlier to check the IP address, you should see it is the new value you assigned:

```
sudo ip addr show
```

In the preceding example we used the `nano` text editing tool. We shall now look at some other options for editing files.

Installing Screen and Vim

Two useful tools to install on your Raspberry Pi 2 are Screen—a terminal multiplexor—and Vim—a text editor.

We will be installing these via a package management tool called apt-get. A package management tool is used for installing extra software onto your operating system. It makes the process easy by keeping track of and downloading any libraries or dependencies needed by the software. It also makes upgrades and removal quite simple.

You can read more about `apt-get` at `http://linux.die.net/man/8/apt-get`.

Before installing Screen and Vim you should update the cache of the `apt-get` repository. This can be done by running the following command:

```
sudo apt-get update
```

We are now ready to install our terminal multiplexor.

We will start by installing Screen. This will allow you to keep multiple bash shells open when you login and out of your Raspberry Pi, so you can leave applications running while you are not directly connected to the device.

 The **Bourne Again Shell** (**bash**) is the shell used in Raspbian by default. You can read more about it here: `https://www.gnu.org/software/bash/`

To install Screen you can use the apt-get package manager:

```
sudo apt-get install screen
```

Once installation is complete, to run Screen you simply type the following command:

```
screen
```

The Screen application will now load, allowing you to create multiple windows containing bash sessions. To create a new window in the screen session type the following command:

```
Ctrl + a then c
```

If you want to remove a window you can kill it. The command to do this is as follows:

```
Ctl + a then k
```

When you have multiple windows open you will want to navigate between them. To move between each open window use the following command:

```
Ctrl + a then num #where num is the screen number, for example 1 or 3
```

To give the screens window a user friendly name type this command:

```
Ctrl + a then Shift + a.
```

This will give you a prompt where you can label the window for ease of use.

To detach from a screen session type the following command:

```
Ctrl + a then d
```

To re-attach you can then type this command:

```
screen -x
```

If more than one screen session is open, type the ID in after the -x, for example:

```
screen -x 1234
```

More information can be found at https://www.gnu.org/software/screen/manual/screen.html.

By default, the Screen application is very plain looking. However, its look and feel can be modified through a .screenrc file.

To learn more about this process, check out the gnu.org site's section on customizing screen at https://www.gnu.org/software/screen/manual/html_node/Customization.html#Customization.

Vim – an optional handy text editor

In addition to the text editors installed by default with Raspbian, you may also wish to install Vim, a powerful text-editing tool. You will see this tool referenced later in this book, so you may find it easier to follow along if you install this.

To install it via our package manager run the following command:

```
sudo apt-get install vim
```

Vim is a complex tool but if you persist with it, you will find it rewarding. A guide can be found here: http://vimhelp.appspot.com/.

Finally, there are a number of other text editors worth exploring if you wish. You can find a list at the official Raspberry Pi website here: https://www.raspberrypi.org/documentation/linux/usage/text-editors.md.

Running tests on the OS and configuration changes

There are ranges of hardware tests we can run on the Raspberry Pi to learn more about it. These include checking voltage readings, the temperature of the device, and testing that the GPIO pins work correctly.

You can run these tests by either connecting to the Pi over SSH or loading up the LXTerminal from the desktop.

Diagnostic tests

The following diagnostic tests provide basic information on your Raspberry Pi. This just provides a taster and many more are available. A more comprehensive list of commands is available via the links at the end of this section.

You should, however, run these tests to get a basic idea of what is possible.

The system information of your Raspberry Pi can be run via the following command:

```
cat /proc/cpuinfo
```

Version information can be seen via the following command:

```
cat /proc/version
```

Memory information can be accessed using the following command:

```
cat /proc/meminfo
```

The microSD cards partitions via the following command:

```
cat /proc/partitions
```

To check the temperature of the device we can use the vcgencmd command:

```
vcgencmd measure_temp
```

We can also use this command with a different parameter to see the voltages. The basic command is as follows:

```
vcgencmd measure_volts id
```

In this command, `id` is one of the following items:

- `core` for the core voltage
- `sdram_c` for the sdram Core voltage
- `sdram_i` for the sdram I/O voltage
- `sdram_p` for the sdram PHY voltage

You can find more commands at elinux.org where a guide to `vcgencmd` can be found (`http://elinux.org/RPI_vcgencmd_usage`).

Over and underclocking the Raspberry Pi

You may want to tweak the performance of your Raspberry Pi 2. This can be achieved by overclocking the device.

Overclocking is the process of forcing the CPU or other component, for example the GPU, to operate faster than its advertised or OS configured clock frequency. In the process of overclocking it is also possible to change the operating voltage to increase the device's speed.

There is a risk associated with overclocking a device, such as instability of its operation or faster degradation of components.

The `raspi-config` menu provides a set of screens to guide you through this process.

You can access `raspi-config` from the command line by typing this command:

```
sudo raspi-config
```

Then you select an overclock option from the menu that is presented.

Alternatively, you can modify the boot configuration file directly from inside the terminal window.

You will need to edit the `/boot/config.txt` file.

Once you have this open you will see a number of commented out values, for example, `#arm_freq=800`.

In the case of our Raspberry Pi 2 the processor runs at 700MHz. We could uncomment this line and up the speed of the processor to 800MHz.

An in-depth guide to overclocking the Raspberry Pi 2 can be found at Hayden James' website: `http://haydenjames.io/raspberry-pi-2-overclock/`.

Going further – testing the GPIO pins

For those interested in exploring diagnostic tools further there is the option of downloading the pigpio GPIO pin test. As you start to work more with the pins this test will come in handy for debugging problems, and allow you to check if you have accidentally damaged a pin.

You can download the pigpio library directly to your Raspberry Pi from `http://abyz.co.uk/rpi/pigpio/download.html`.

An overview and instructions on use can be found at `http://abyz.co.uk/rpi/pigpio/index.html`.

Example applications and tests can be found at `http://abyz.co.uk/rpi/pigpio/examples.html`.

For those looking for a digital waveform view for the Raspberry Pi's GPIO pins you can install piscope from `http://abyz.co.uk/rpi/pigpio/piscope.html`.

Some handy Linux commands

The following Linux commands are very useful and you will find yourself using them often. Remember you can type `man command` where `command` is the command you are interested in at any time to learn more about it and the parameters it accepts.

> Most commands also contain a more concise set of documentation under `help` as well.

The `cd` command allows you to change directories:

```
cd /home/pi
```

The `touch` command creates an empty file:

```
touch test.txt
```

The `cp` command can be used to copy files:

```
cp  /home/pi/test.txt /home/newuser/test.txt
```

The `mv` command can be used to move a file or rename a file:

```
mv /home/pi/test.txt /home/pi/test2.txt
```

The `rm` command will remove a file or directory depending on the flag used:

```
rm text.txt
```

To find out which directory you are in you can use the `pwd` (present working directory) command:

```
pwd
```

If you wish to list the contents of a directory you can use the `ls` command:

```
ls
```

To learn more about basic Linux commands, the Debian operating system website provides a in-depth guide at `https://www.debian.org/doc/manuals/user/ch6.html`.

Troubleshooting

You may from time to time hit problems in your setup or when running software or hardware with your Raspberry Pi 2. A good first place to check for help is the eLinux Raspberry Pi troubleshooting page at `http://elinux.org/R-Pi_Troubleshooting`.

As well as this site, the official Raspberry Pi website has an active and friendly forum where you can post questions for help at `https://www.raspberrypi.org/forums/`.

Finally, the Raspberry Pi section of Stack Exchange is another great resource, at`http://raspberrypi.stackexchange.com/`.

Summary

In this chapter we learned about the basics of the Raspberry Pi 2's hardware. We discovered how to setup a microSD card and install the Raspbian operating system on it.

Following this, we created RSA keys to access our RPI over SSH and installed a number of useful tools via a package manager and experimented with some diagnostic tests.

With our Raspberry Pi 2 setup and ready to go we can now move onto writing applications that work on the device.

Programming on Raspbian

2

In this chapter we will start to examine programming on the Raspbian operating system. This will give you the chance to explore the Raspberry Pi's hardware in more detail and interact with some of its components.

The topics covered in this chapter include the following:

- Assembly language and the assembler
- An introduction to the C and C++ languages and their compilers
- The Python programming language and IDLE

Each of these topics will lay the foundation for projects in future chapters. For this chapter you will need to either be logged into your Raspberry Pi via SSH or have a terminal window open.

Which programming languages?

There is a plethora of programming languages available on the Raspberry Pi, so knowing where to start can be hard. Many languages are useful for a variety of different project types, including building websites, programming hardware, and writing desktop applications.

In this book we will use Assembly, C/C++, and Python. Each of these languages provides us with methods for exploring different aspects of the Raspberry Pi.

Assembly language, being so close to the computer's hardware, will help you to explore more about computer architecture and how it is realized on the Raspberry Pi. You'll also have the benefit that some of steps needed to build your executable in Assembly carry over to C and C++.

The C/C++ languages are popular for building software for controlling external electronics hardware and in the case of C, are the language Raspbian is written in. Using the knowledge you gain about Assembly, you'll be able to start tackling C programs next.

Finally, the Python programming language is incredibly versatile. From writing web servers to controlling hardware, you'll find it a useful tool for your future projects. The understanding of the C language you will gain will help to shed some light onto Python.

The first language we are going to start with is Assembly language, so login to your Raspberry Pi and get ready to write some code.

Assembly language

The Raspberry Pi comes equipped with an ARM v7 quad core processor. Each processor has its own set of specific machine code that it understands; this machine code is represented in binary format. The machine code is different for each processor architecture, so the Raspberry Pi's ARM processor machine code will not work on an IBM or Intel CPU.

Short of writing out 32-bit binary machine code instructions, the lowest level of programming language we can find ourselves using is Assembler language, also known as Assembly language.

The computer architecture's Assembly language is usually a one-to-one mapping between itself and the underlying machine code. This is achieved through using a mnemonic. A combination of these mnemonic codes will result in an operation such as addition or subtraction.

A program written in Assembly language is compiled into machine code by the Assembler program. This program passes through the code one or more times and generates an object file as part of this process. The Assembler in some cases will also perform a variety of optimizations on the code in its subsequent passes.

Following this, a program called the **Linker** generates an executable file you can run on your computer.

Two important terms you will come across when writing Assembly language are **opcode** and **operand**. The opcode is an instruction (such as add) and the operand is data (such as an integer value). Each opcode and operand is created through the combination of sets of 8 bits (1 byte).

In this chapter we will write a simple program in Assembly language in order to understand the basics. The subject of the ARM v7 Assembly language is covered in more detail in later chapters; however, the University of Michigan hosts a useful guide to the ARM v7 architecture in PDF format at `https://web.eecs.umich.edu/~prabal/teaching/eecs373-f10/readings/ARMv7-M_ARM.pdf`.

You maybe interested in reviewing this as a supplement to the topics covered here.

So what do the mnemonic codes that make up Assembly language look like before being converted to machine code?

Let's take a look at an example and see. Here we demonstrate how we can take register 0 of the CPU and assign a number to it, in this case, `10`.

```
MOV R0, #10
```

In Assembly code, `MOV` is short hand for assigning a value. The register is an example of the processor's internal memory storage location and of course `10` is an integer value.

> You can read more on CPU registers at Wikipedia: `https://en.wikipedia.org/wiki/Processor_register`

As you explore the language further you will become familiar with these types of command, as they are the building blocks of your program.

How about looking at another example? What do you think this does?

```
ADD R0, R1, R2
```

This simple program introduces us to another mnemonic, `ADD`. Here we are taking the values of registers 1 and 2, adding them, and assigning them to register 0.

Running commands like this on the Raspberry Pi is very simple; we can add them to a file assemble and link them ourselves.

We shall now explore a short Assembly language program that incorporates these two commands, `MOV` and `ADD`.

Let's start by creating a new directory under the `pi` user:

```
mkdir /home/pi/assem_programs
```

This will be the place we store our Assembly code.

Navigate into this directory:

```
cd /home/pi/assem_programs
```

Next we need to create a new file to place our code in. You can choose any text editor you are comfortable with in order to write the program. We have used Vim in the following example:

```
vim first_assem_prog.s
```

To this file add the following block of code. Make sure that you include the spacing as demonstrated below:

```
        .global main
        .func main
main:
        MOV R0, #0
        MOV R1, #10
        MOV R2, #20
        ADD R0, R1, R2
        BX LR
```

So what does this program do?

The first line in the program defines a directive called `main`. The prefix of `.global` tells the Assembler that the name is global and thus available to the C runtime.

 A directive is code executed by the Assembler at assembly time, rather than the processor. We could have called this directive anything but have gone with `main` to keep it consistent with our C program. Assembler, unlike C, does not require the program entry point to be called `main`.

As you will see, we will use the GCC compiler/linker to build an executable for our program, so the format we are writing the Assembly language in mimics that of a C program in some areas. This is why you will see references to the C runtime mentioned when discussing Assembly in this chapter.

Following this, we then define that `main` is a function. Here we can see another directive, called `.func`, is used to specify this.

So now we have `main` available we can denote where this function starts, which in our case is the third line.

Contained in the function are three lines of code for adding values to the registers. These should be familiar from our earlier examples. What we have done is assigned the value 0 to R0, 10 to R1, 20 to R2 and then added the values together and stored the result (30) in R0.

Finally, we call BX LR to return the value of register 0 back to the operating system.

As you can see this program is very simple, but it demonstrates how to add numbers and store the results.

Save the file and exit your text editor. You should now be back at the command line.

This leads us to the next step of assembling and linking in order to generate a file we can run.

Assembling and linking

Now we have a program we need to test. This is a two-step process that involves assembling the code and then linking it, which we touched upon at the start of this section. We will also explain these two items in more technical detail later in this book, but for this chapter it will suffice to understand roughly what they do and how to run them.

When you come to explore the C language next, you will see linking is also a component there as well; in fact, we use the same tool for both C and Assembly—the GCC compiler.

Briefly, these two steps to generate a runnable program can be summed up as follows:

- Assembling is the process of generating the machine code object file from the Assembly mnemonics
- Linking is the process of creating an executable from one or more object files

The first command we will run, called as(the GNU assembler), will take the code we wrote previously and create an object file as its output.

Run the following command from inside the folder where you created your program:

```
as -o first_assem_prog.o first_assem_prog.s
```

If it assembled correctly, you should see no output.

Following this we need to run the linker, which is invoked with the `gcc` command. There is also another linker available, called `ld`. However, since we are writing our Assembly in a C-like manner, use the `gcc` tool.

You will also need to run this command in the same directory that you ran `as` in.

```
gcc -o first_assem_prog first_assem_prog.o
```

[GCC stands for the GNU Compiler Collection.]

If everything is successful, you shouldn't see any output.

We now have an executable file we can run from the Linux command line.

To do this you can simply type this command:

```
./first_assem_prog
```

You'll notice there is no output, however. So how do we know the program executed correctly?

We can use the Linux `echo` command, as follows:

```
echo $?
```

This displays the exit code of the previous process, which in our case is the result of program we just ran. You may remember that we wrote this value using the `BX LR` code.

As our program simply returned a value of 30 to register 0, this is the result we can see when using the `echo` command.

You can try changing the values in your program and assembling and linking once more. The result you see when running echo should reflect your changes.

[Try changing the program to use R1 instead of R0 in the `add` function and see what happens.]

So in a few easy steps you have created an Assembly language program and learned how to assemble, link, and run it.

This forms the basics you will need in order to tackle the more complex programs in the next chapter, where we will discuss the language in more depth.

Now we have our first program under our belt, let's move on to take a look at the C and C++ languages and explore GCC further.

The C and C++ languages

Even if you are new to programming you may have come across C and C++ mentioned in literature, webpages, and text books. You'll often see C/C++ written. However, it is important to realize that while C++ is based upon C they are indeed different languages, and useful in different contexts.

We are going to start by giving a brief overview of these languages and explain a bit about them. Following this we will write some experimental programs and explore how the compiler works.

Let's start by delving a bit further into C.

C – a brief introduction

The C programming language has been around since 1970s and was closely tied with the development of the Unix operating system.

In 1972, the computer scientist Dennis Ritchie started the development of C in Assembly language on the PDP-11 Unix system. As we demonstrated in the previous section, Assembly language is converted to machine code, and Ritchie's C language represented another level of abstraction from the computer hardware and Assembly itself.

Shortly after, in February 1973, the C language could be found bundled with the Unix release and available for developers.

In the 1980s, due to its widespread adoption, the American National Standards Institute (ANSI) formed a committee known as X3J11 to adopt a standard for the C programming language. This would help to govern the direction of the language and formalize its specifications.

By 1990 the C standard championed by ANSI was adopted by the International Organization for Standardization (ISO) who would then help to steer its future path.

From these early days the C language has gone through several revisions and been ported to many computer architectures, including Linux on the Raspberry Pi 2. It has thus become a popular choice for application development due to its ubiquitous nature.

The Linux operating system, of which Raspbian is a flavor, is written in the C language. Therefore, if you wish to write applications at the operating system level, having a good command of the C language is invaluable.

One of the great features of C and a contributing factor to why it is popular for embedded device software development is its speed. Most C implementations are compiled directly to machine code and the software engineer has full control over what happens at the hardware level.

Later in this book we cover hardware development and programming, and the C language is something you will encounter when working on these projects.

Now that we have briefly touched upon C, let's take a look at C++.

A quick look at C++

The C++ programming language's origins can be found in the late 1970s with Danish computer scientist Bjarne Stroustrup. Stroustrup looked to implement a version of the C programming language that incorporated object-oriented features from the Simula programming language, such as classes.

At first, the language was known as C with classes and in 1983 adopted the name we are all familiar with, C++.

Throughout the 1980s, the book *The C++ Programming Language* acted as the main reference guide to the language. Following this the language went through several revisions and was adopted as an ISO standard in 1998.

While C++ is based upon C it does contain some notable differences due to not retaining complete source level compatibility with the original C language.

For those interested in a further look at these differences you can find a summary on Wikipedia at `https://en.wikipedia.org/wiki/Compatibility_of_C_and_C%2B%2B`.

Where C++ also differs from C is its inclusion of many OOP features such as the following:

- Classes
- Interfaces and abstract classes
- Objects
- Inheritance

You may be wondering why we are interested in both C and C++. After all, if the operating system is written in C, and C is good for many electronic projects, why look at C++?As you will discover in the Raspberry Pi world, hardware such as the Raspberry Pi to Arduino Connection Bridge uses a C++-based library.

Therefore, familiarizing yourself with the language will help you to implement third party libraries that contain many interesting features and functionality.

As we noted, since C++ is based upon the C language, in this chapter we will start by writing a simple C program only.

This will give you an introduction to the basic structure of a program and header files. In future chapters we will expand upon this to include C++ libraries, explore the differences between the languages when relevant, and look at how to include C header files in a C++ application.

Let's now delve into writing our first C application.

Our first C program

In order to write our first program we need three key things. These are similar to those needed when writing our Assembly language program:

- A good text editor such as Vim
- C libraries of re-usable code
- The C compiler

The text editor you use will largely be driven by your own tastes. In the previous chapter of this book we briefly looked at Vim and also linked to a number of other text editors recommended on the Raspberry Pi website.

When writing our Assembly language application, you were presented the choice of using whichever editor you were comfortable with.

Another popular GUI-based text editor you may be interested in using is Geany. Feel free to skip this section if you would prefer not to use this editor.

Geany – a handy text editor and development environment

The Geany text editing environment provides support for integrating development tools such as Makefiles and compilers and provides a neat GUI for editing code files. This integration can help when you start to work on larger projects.

For example, you can hook up the GCC compiler to work in Geany and thus compile your applications and test them from within the text editor.

 Makefiles are a way of combining many commands, such as those needed to compile projects into a single file. These can then be run from the command line using the **make** application. You can read more on make at `http://man7.org/linux/man-pages/man1/make.1.html`.

If you are interested in testing this out, you can install it via the package manager:

```
sudo apt-get install geany
```

More information on the editor and its development tool support can be found at `http://www.geany.org/Documentation/Manual`.

Now, with whichever text editor you have chosen we are going to create a new C program. This will help us to explore the second and third bullet point from our previous list.

Creating a new C program

Our first task is to create a new folder on the Raspberry Pi 2 to store our source code in.

In the exercise in this section of the chapter we will store the code in a directory called `c_programs`. You can create this under the Pi user as follows:

```
mkdir /home/pi/c_programs
```

Once you have this directory created we can write our C program. Using whichever text editor you prefer, create a file called `first_c_prog.c`. For example, if you were using Vim, you would create the file as follows:

```
vim /home/pi/c_programs/first_c_prog.c
```

Users of Geany can create a new file from directly inside the IDE.

The following program demonstrates how we can enter a value into our program via the keyboard and then display it back to the user. Let's start by adding the first line at the top of the file:

```
#include <stdio.h>
```

This is an example of an include statement. Here we are telling the program to use the `stdio.h` library. This library contains standard input and output functions. Examples of functions in this program we will be using from this library include `printf()` and `scanf()`. The next section of this chapter explains libraries in more detail. So for the moment let's move on and add the main body of our program:

```
int main(void)
{
  int a;
  printf("Please input an integer: ");
  scanf("%d", &a);
  printf("You entered the number: %d\n", a);
  return 0;
}
```

Each C program needs to contain a `main()` function. You'll remember from your Assembly program we also had a function called `main`. This is the entry point of the program.

The signature of our function is as follows:

```
int main(void)
```

This tells us that the main function has no variables passed to it but returns an integer value when it has finished running.

Within the braces of the program we have five lines of code.

The first line defines an integer variable with the name `a`. The second line uses a function that is included from the `stdio.h` library called `printf()`. This function allows us to print text to the screen.

In our case we are prompting the user to enter an integer value.

Following this, the `scanf()` function is used to take user input from the keyboard and store it in the `a` variable.

The `%d` you can see in the function tells us that the function is expecting an integer. Here we can also see the reference to the variable `a` uses the `&` symbol. In this instance, `&` is used to tell the `scanf()` function the location of the variable, rather than the variable's value.

The next thing we want to do is print out the value entered. This is done using the `printf()` function once again. Here we use `%d` to say we want to output an integer as part of the string. `\n` is used to denote a new line. Finally, you can see the `a` variable is included. This time we want its actual value so we do not include the `&`.

The value of a is then inserted into the string where %d is when the string is displayed.

The final line of code before the closing brace is the return statement. The return statement contains the integer 0 after it (and is why we prefixed int to the function name). This means our program executed without a problem, so we return 0 to show there is no error code.

In our Assembly program we returned the value 30. As you will see, this 0 value is also available via the echo command we were introduced to earlier.

Before running this program, we are going to return to the top of our program and explore libraries further.

C libraries – a trove of reusable code

As you saw in our first C program we included a header file: stdio.h.

Within the C language, many problems have already been solved, for example, how to take input from the keyboard and print it to the screen. These solved problems are then packaged as C code libraries and can be included via .h files, thus sharing the code between multiple source files.

Header files can be written by either the programmer working on a project, or included in the default system code that comes bundled with your operating system.

To include a header in your application you use the include statement, #include.

There are then two formats for how you specify the library to include. One uses angular brackets (<) and the other uses quotation marks (").

When you are including a system header such as stdio.h, then use angular brackets:

```
#include <stdio.h>
```

The compiler will then look in a list of standard system directories such as /usr/lib.

If you wish to include a header file you wrote yourself, then use quotations:

```
#include "mylib.h"
```

You can find a comprehensive list of system level header files at http://en.cppreference.com/w/c/header.

Strictly speaking, the header file tells the C compiler certain things, such as function declarations, but does not contain their definitions. The library file however contains the actual executable code referenced in the header file. When we explore the C compiler in the next section, we will explain how we include the executable code via the linker.

The simplest way to think of this is: the header tells us what exists and the library contains the code that does it.

The C (and C++) compiler

We now have the source code for our small program, but until it has been compiled it can't be run.

The compiler performs the task of taking a high level language such as C and decoding it into machine code. This machine code can then be read by the processor and is how the computer executes our program.

However, even after we have compiled our program successfully, it is still not ready to be run. There is another stage we need to consider—linking. You will recognize this from our earlier Assembly language program.

The linker is an important part of the process of building a C-based executable. It is responsible for taking separate object files and linking them together in order to create a single executable. This methodology allows us to take a compiled third party library, reference it in our code, and then include it via the linking method. Thus we do not need to recompile the third party library along with our code.

Unlike the steps required for Assembly, the preceding can usually be performed in a single command, which handles the linking and machine code generation.

In fact, the process of building an executable is even more complex than we have touched upon here. However, for the program you will be writing, understanding you need to invoke the compiler and link to third party objects should be sufficient.

For those interested in reading further can visit `http://www.tenouk.com/ModuleW.html`, which provides a greater breakdown.

As you saw previously, the GCC compiler is installed by default on Raspbian. You can read more about it at the gnu.org website, `https://gcc.gnu.org/`.

The GCC compiler supports a number of languages other than Assembly including C and C++. When we wish to compile a program we can use the `gcc` command in the terminal window to invoke the compiler.

You will be familiar with this from using it in the linking stage in your first Assembly program.

As you come to use the compiler there are a number of items you need to consider. These include the following:

- The input file that is your C code
- The output file that is your compiled program
- Options for the linker to tell it which libraries to include

Taking the program we wrote, `first_c_prog.c`, we will now compile and run it so you can see `gcc` in action and explore the preceding bullet points.

Compiling and running our application

The following instructions assume you saved your C code into the `c_programs` directory.

Navigate into this directory:

```
cd /home/pi/c_programs
```

From here we will now invoke the GCC compiler using the following command:

```
gcc -o first_c_prog first_c_prog.c
```

This command is very simple, and we have not had to specify the linker. You may be wondering why this is, considering the fact we included the `stdio` header.

This is because certain functions are linked by default, such as those in `libc`, therefore we do not need to manually link them. As you explore the C language further, however, you will quickly come across instances where you have to link.

You can check which headers are available from the C standard library in each version of the C language at `https://en.wikipedia.org/wiki/C_standard_library`.

In this command we have addressed the first bullet point in the list, the input file that is our program. In our command it is the last parameter we pass in.

As we stated, we do not need to add any references to the linker, which would be the third bullet point.

Finally, the second bullet point is covered by `-o first_c_prog`, which tells us to output the executable called `first_c_prog`.

If you run `ls` in the directory, you should see the `first_c_prog` file.

You can now run this by typing:

```
./first_c_prog
```

If this executed successfully, you will be prompted to enter an integer. Once entering this you will see it output to the screen.

 Try entering a non-integer such as an alphabet character and see what happens.

This concludes writing our first C program. Hopefully you will agree it was fairly easy to write!

Next we will look at the Python programming language. Python is a handy scripting and object-oriented programming language and uses C as its base, as you will see.

The Python language

Software Engineer Guido van Rossum founded what would come to be known as the Python programming language in the late 1980s. Spawned from a project he was working on to develop an interpreter for a scripting language, he chose the working title Python derived from the popular British comedy series Monty Python's Flying Circus.

The official Python website can be found at `https://www.python.org/`.

Unlike the C language, Python is an interpreted language. This in essence means that the language's instructions are performed by an interpreter rather than compiled down to machine code.

You can read more about interpreted languages here `https://en.wikibooks.org/wiki/Introduction_to_Programming_Languages/Interpreted_Programs`.

The most widely used implementation of the Python language is known as CPython, which is written in C. This is also the implementation you will be using on the Raspbian operating system.

You can read more about this implementation at `https://docs.python.org/2/c-api/`.

This means the Python language is also extensible via C and C++. The Python website provides a guide to extending its functionality at `https://docs.python.org/2/extending/extending.html`.

The two popular versions of the language are version 2 and version 3.

There are some backward incompatibility issues between version 3 and 2 of the language. Currently, version 2 has wider adoption. In this book we will therefore be using version 2. Version 2 also comes shipped by default with Raspbian.

Let's now take a look at writing a simple application that performs a similar task to that of the C program we just completed.

A simple Python program

We are going to start by opening the IDLE Python development tool. **IDLE** stands for Integrated DeveLopment Environment and is the program you can use on your Raspberry Pi to directly write Python applications and run them.

At the command line, type the following command:

`python`

Once loaded you will see a blank document with some information about the version of Python displayed at the top. The following screenshot shows an example:

```
pi@raspberrypi ~ $ python
Python 2.7.3 (default, Mar 18 2014, 05:13:23)
[GCC 4.6.3] on linux2
Type "help", "copyright", "credits" or "license" for more information.
>>>
```

Example of IDLE on the Raspberry Pi.

In Python, white spacing is very important. Unlike C we do not use braces to signify the start and end of a function, but rather white space indentation.

In our example programs we will use four spaces of indentation.

Our first simple program contains a prompt to the user to enter an integer and then outputs it.

Type the following into IDLE:

```
def main():
    a = raw_input("Please enter an integer: ");
    print "You entered the number : ", a
```

When you have finished adding the code, press the *Return* key twice. You will now see the prompt again.

Into this, type the following command:

```
main()
```

You should now be requested for input. Enter a number, for example, 8, and then press *Return*.

This number should now be displayed with the message You entered the number: prefixing it. This was even easier to write and execute than the Assembly and C program: we needed less code and did not have to run a compiler or linker!

Let's take a look at what each section of the program does.

The first piece of code we entered was the function signature. This has some similarities to the C program we wrote, in that it is called main.

However, unlike the C program, we could have called this anything, for example hello().

If you wish, try re-entering the program with a different name for the function and execute it again. You'll see that it still works.

Following the function definition, we define a variable called a. Python does not force us to define the variable type (for example int) via a prefix when we declare it. We can simply give the variable a name and that will suffice.

The raw_input() function prompts the user and assigns the value typed in by the user to the a variable.

Following this, we output the user's input using the print statement. Therefore, in three lines we have achieved that which took eight in C.

Another interesting property of our program is that unlike our C program we can type any value we want into the prompt, whether it is an integer or not.

You can try this for yourself and see what happens.

While using IDLE is great, if we shut down IDLE our program vanishes. So how do we get around that?

Running a Python program from a file

As we develop projects for our Raspberry Pi we want to be able to save our programs into a file and execute them this way. This allows for re-use. We also may not want to use IDLE but our favorite text editor.

Thankfully we can and shall now walk through the steps to do this.

Create a new directory under your `/home/pi/` user called `python_programs`.

Into this we are going create a new file called `first_python_prog.py`.

For example, you can use the `touch` command to create an empty file:

```
touch first_python_prog.py
```

Open this file up in your text editor and copy the code in from our earlier example. This will be the code you typed into IDLE.

Once complete at the top of your file you will need to add the shebang:

```
#!/usr/bin/python
```

The shebang contains the path to the version of Python being run. This allows the script to be standalone without having to type `python` before it as you will see shortly.

To the bottom of the file you will also need to add the following:

```
if __name__ == '__main__':
    main()
```

This piece of code checks to see if the Python interpreter has set the __name__ variable to __main__, meaning that the program being run is the main program. If this is true, then it executes the `main()` function. We did not have to call our function `main`. Unlike C, Python will allow you to name the entry point to your program anything you like. However, for consistency in our projects we will use the name `main`.

You can read more about Python runtime services on the official website, where __main__ is also touched upon, at `https://docs.python.org/2/library/python.html`.

Having added the code, the file should look as follows:

```
#!/usr/bin/python

def main():
```

```
    a = raw_input("Please enter an integer: ");
    print "You entered the number: ", a


 if __name__ == '__main__':
    main()
```

Save this code and return to the command line.

To run the application, we can simply type the following command:

`python first_python_prog.py`

You should now see on the screen a prompt to enter some text. Add this and press *return* and it will be output back to you.

As with the earlier example of this program, the application will take text characters as well as integers.

We mentioned that the shebang means we do not need to add the command `python` before running the script. However, before we can simply execute the file from the command line we need to set the permissions on the file to allow it to execute.

In the terminal type this command:

`chmod +x first_python_prog.py`

Now you can try running the script again by typing the following:

`./first_python_prog.py`

Once again the prompt should appear.

 You can read more about chmod here: `https://en.wikipedia.org/wiki/Chmod`

This wraps up our Python section. Here we created the same program in Python as we did in C to compare the complexity and syntax.

We will explore the Python language further in future chapters in which we build a web server.

Let's now review what we have learned so far.

Summary

In this chapter we explored the programming languages we will be using in this book. This included Assembler, C/C++ and Python.

A guide to writing a small Assembly language program was shared, and we then assembled and linked our program.

Following this, we learned some basics of how to write a C application and how to compile and run it. Also discussed were some of the similarities between Assembly language and C when it comes to generating an executable file.

The last program we explored was Python. Here you learned to write a program that contained the same functionality as your C program in the Python IDLE.

Following this, we moved our program into a file and demonstrated how it can be run standalone.

The tasks performed over the course of this chapter will lay the foundation for future projects where we build upon these skills.

So what's next? In the next chapter we will discuss the Assembly language in more detail and start to write some interesting programs with it.

3
Low-Level Development with Assembly Language

Now you have had the chance to write a basic program in Assembly language, it is time to dive into the subject in more detail.

In this chapter we will learn more about:

- The assembler
- The GNU compiler
- Branching
- Comments
- Memory
- Addresses
- Control structures
- Makefiles

These will help to give you a better understanding of the ARM architecture that the Raspberry Pi 2 uses.

First of all, let's go back to basics and explore some of the items we touched upon in the previous chapter in more detail.

Back to basics

In the previous chapter we wrote a simple program that introduced a handful of Assembly language mnemonics and showed us how to assemble and link a program.

This introduction program was written in ARM Assembly language, ARM being the type of CPU architecture the Raspberry Pi 2 contains. **Acorn RISC Machine (ARM)** implements RISC, which stands for **Reduced Instruction Set Computing**. This results in a smaller optimized set of machine code, which in turn leads to a smaller but expressive Assembly language.

If you wish to understand the subject further you can read more about RISC on Wikipedia at `https://en.wikipedia.org/wiki/Reduced_instruction_set_computing`.

The next program we will write is very similar to that in the previous chapter, but slightly simpler.

Make sure you are logged into your Raspberry Pi over SSH or have a terminal window open in Raspbian.

Create a new file in your `assem_programs` directory called `second_assem_prog.s`.

Create the file as follows:

`vim /home/pi/assem_programs/second_assem_prog.s`

Into this file add the following code:

```
/* second_assem_prog */
.global main
.func main
main:
    MOV R0, #7 @Add 7 to register 0
    BX LR
```

Let's walk through this and look at each line in detail. You should be familiar with some of the commands now, but we have added some new syntax as well.

> An interesting fact about Assembly language is that commands such as MOV and references to registers such as R0 can also be written in lower case as well.
>
> For example, MOV could be written as mov. For ease of reading and to distinguish comments and directives from commands we will use a convention of uppercase when referencing commands, registers, and similar, and lowercase for directives and comments.

Multiline comments

The first item you will see is the value/* `second_assem_prog` */. What we have done here is wrapped a plain text English string in /*and */. This is known as a comment block.

Comment blocks allow us to add text to annotate our programs in plain English (or whichever language you speak) to provide information to other programmers on why a program performs a certain task.

If you have programmed in other languages, you may already be familiar with this concept. As you come to write programs in C and C++ you will also encounter the use of comments, which like Assembly language can be wrapped in /* and */.

When the assembler processes the code in our program it knows to ignore any text located in the comment blocks. So as long as you have wrapped the text correctly inside the symbols you can include any information you think makes sense.

Following the comment block we have two examples of directives. These are `.global` main and `.func` main.

We touched upon these briefly in the first chapter, where we explained they were written C style. Now we shall go into more detail.

Directives

A directive in Assembly language is a command that is part of the ARM assembly syntax but is not part of the CPU's instruction set. Therefore, it does not have a one-to-one mapping. You will therefore sometimes see directives referenced as pseudo-op codes. Unlike a regular opcode such as the binary representation of MOV, a directive is referenced by the assembler, but not by the CPU at runtime.

Common practice is to denote a directive using "." beforehand and to write it in lower case. In our example program you can see this with the `.global` and `.func` directives.

Some of the benefits of directives include the following:

- Making a program easier to read for the engineers working on it
- Reserving memory and initializing the value of it prior to runtime
- Making the assembly of a program reliant upon input, thus allowing for a developer to implement multiple assembly options based upon environment or application

The reason we use C-style directives is we can then use the C runtime to handle the initialization step and termination step of the application.

The initialization step includes calling the `main` function. As you will remember when we wrote our C application in *Chapter 2, Programming on Raspbian*, we had to include this function to specify the start of the program.

Let's now take a look at this line:

```
MOV R0, #7 @Add 7 to register 0
```

You'll see something new here. Let's explore this further.

Single line comments

This should look familiar to you. Here we are moving an integer, 7, into register 0. However, at the end of the line you will see we have added a plain text prefix with the @ symbol.

The @ symbol can also be used for comments. However, in this case it only takes a single line. If you wish to comment more than one line you will need to use a multiline comment block.

We know from the previous chapter that a register is a form of memory available to the CPU; however, let's look at this in more detail.

Registers

The registers found on a CPU are small storage units that contain the operands of our programs.

These registers are divided up into different types, depending on the type of number we are saving to them. There are floating point registers and integer registers.

You will see these referenced in our programs in the following format: R0, R1, through to R15.

We can use mathematical operations such as ADD, SUB, and MOV to set the value of the register.

For more information on the ARM architecture and the registers, you can refer to the ARM website: http://infocenter.arm.com/help/index.jsp?topic=/com.arm.doc.subset.cortexa.cortexa7/index.html.

You'll get used to using registers a lot when writing Assembly programs. One important register reference is LR, which we will explore with regard to branching.

Branching

The final line of our application handles the branching and exchange:

```
BX LR
```

The branching and exchange portion of the command (BX) means that we change the sequential execution by branching to the LR register. Branching allows us to switch from one sequential path to another, if, for example, a state changes.

In the case of our program, this branching results in us exiting the main function and terminates our program.

The LR portion of this command is a special register that contains the address the program returns to when a function is complete. In our case, this will be the register to return to once main has finished executing.

Further on in this chapter you will see how you can use branching within your program. This will allow you to jump to another block of code when a condition is met.

The assembler

In the previous chapter we briefly touched upon the portable GNU assembler, which was activated via the as command.

The assembler is a powerful tool that supports many options, most of which are out of scope of this book.

For further information on the tool you can refer to the GNU assembler man page at http://linux.die.net/man/1/as.

You can also access the man pages by typing the following command:

```
man as
```

The man command loads the manual for the tool passed into it. You will find that many Linux applications contain a manual.

So at its heart, what does the Assembler do?

First of all, the program takes each mnemonic and converts it into the correct machine code representation.

For example, MOV R4, R1 could be represented in binary as follows:

```
1110 0001 1010 0000 0100 0000 0000 0001
```

A handy guide to how the binary maps to the ARM instruction set can be found at `http://stackoverflow.com/questions/11785973/converting-very-simple-arm-instructions-to-binary-hex`.

The preceding code could also be presented in Hexadecimal format as follows:

```
E1A04001
```

This process will also pick up on syntax mistakes in your program and throw an error if it comes across a mnemonic that is not part of its set.

You define where the output of the `as` command is stored using the `-o` flag. This file, known as the object file, is then passed into the linker for the creation of the final executable.

The linker

After you have generated your object file you are now ready to generate an executable file that can be run within the Linux operating system. You'll remember from the earlier chapter that the `gcc` command was used.

You may also remember we briefly mentioned that an `ld` command exits, the GNU linker. The `gcc` compiler actually acts as a frontend or wrapper to the `ld` command.

It also provides us with a handy set of flags we can use when linking our object files. One example is as follows:

```
-v
```

The `v` is short for verbose and this will print out all of the commands that are run during the linking phase.

As you come to use the linker more you may find using the `v` flag is useful, especially if multiple files are being linked to create a single executable.

You can read more about the GCC compiler, including a guide to many of its flags, at `https://gcc.gnu.org/wiki/Building_Cross_Toolchains_with_gcc?action=AttachFile&do=get&target=billgatliff-toolchains.pdf`.

Makefiles

When we completed the program in the previous chapter we ran the two commands we just discussed, the assembler and linker.

This process can be tedious, especially if we have multiple files to link and other steps to perform. Thankfully there is an easier method, so here we introduce you to Makefiles.

The command `Make` is a utility you can use for maintaining programs by chaining together multiple commands and compilation directives in a single file. The `Make` command will process this file, called a **Makefile**.

The `Make` command man page can found online here: `http://linux.die.net/man/1/make`.

It can also be found by running this command:

```
man make
```

We will now create a simple `Makefile` to demonstrate how this process works. This file will be responsible for containing the assembly and link instructions for the program at the beginning of this chapter.

Start by navigating into the `assem_programs` directory if you are not already there.

We are now going to create a new file called `Makefile` using whichever text editor you are comfortable with:

```
vim Makefile
```

Add the following lines to this file:

```
all: second_assem_prog
second_assem_prog: second_assem_prog.o
                gcc -o $@ $+
second_assem_prog.o: second_assem_prog.s
                as -o $@ $<
```

Let's take a look at what each of these statements does.

The top line kicks off the program. When we run `make`, this is the first command to be executed. What it does is say "run the second line."

The second line then calls the third, which uses the assembler to generate the object file. This object file is then passed back to the second line as input, which then runs the `gcc` command.

Finally, the executable is output and the `make` application exits.

Save this file and exit your text editor.

We can now test that this works by simply running the following command:

```
make
```

Once the command has completed you should see your generated `second_assem_prog` file.

Try running this command:

```
./second_assem_prog
```

Then check, using the `echo` command, that the value `7` is output:

```
echo $?
```

> The `Make` man page includes a list of the flags it is also possible to use when running Makefiles. You may find some of these useful to experiment with including the `-d` flag for debugging. You can also try adding in the `-v` flag and running the `Makefile` again.

Going forward, you can use this `Makefile` as a template for other programs, updating the labels as necessary, and adding further bash commands as required.

The `Makefile` can of course also be used for Python and C programs. In the case of a C program, the `Makefile` will also be used to invoke the `gcc` command.

This concludes a review of the basics. Let's now write a more complex program so we can explore the Assembly language further.

Memory and addresses

In this section, we will write a program that subtracts the value of one register from another and stores the result in register `0`.

In order to do this, we will create a number of variables with integers that are then assigned to the register. This will introduce you to the concepts of memory and addresses. During this process you will also understand a few new terms that are important to the Assembly language.

We will use the following program to explore these items:

```
.data
/* Variable definition */
.balign 4
wordvar1:
    .word 7
.balign 4
wordvar2:
    .word 3
```

```
.text
/* code definition */
.balign 4
.global main
main:
    LDR R1, wordvar1addr
    LDR R1, [R1]
    LDR R2, wordvar2addr
    LDR R2, [R2]
    SUB R0, R1, R2 @ Subtract 3 from 7
    BX LR

wordvar1addr : .word wordvar1
wordvar2addr : .word wordvar2
```

Add this program to a new file called `third_assem_prog.s` and save it.

This should be stored with the other Assembly programs you created in the `assem_programs` directory.

Let's look at the new features we have introduced.

The .data directive

The first new feature compared to our earlier two programs is a new definition at the top of the file called `data`:

```
.data
/* Variable definition */
.balign 4
wordvar1:
    .word 7
.balign 4
wordvar2:
    .word 3
```

The period (.) should alert you that `.data` is a directive. Under this directive we have a chunk of code that contains `.word`, labels, and `.balign`.

These are used to define variables and the data for our program in advance.

Each of these items will be discussed in more detail.

The .balign directive

A `.balign` directive is used to make sure that the next piece of data or instruction is a multiple of 4 bytes.

The ARM architecture restricts the types of address of data you can use. You can read more about `.balign` at `https://sourceware.org/binutils/docs/as/Balign.html`.

The next piece of data we will be storing will be 32bits long. We will now look at this.

Words

A word in Assembly language actually refers to a 32-bit (4-byte) integer. Therefore, when using the `.word` directive we are telling the assembler that it should represent the value as a 32-bit value.

In the following block of code we are defining a 4-byte integer with the value 7:

```
wordvar1:
    .word 7
```

The value 7 would be represented in binary format as:

```
0000 0000 0000 0111
```

This word with the value 7 is stored as a variable with the label `wordvar1`. Let's now take a look at labels in a little more detail.

Labels

In the previous section we discussed how `wordvar1` was a label. There are some further examples in the program, including the following code:

```
wordvar2addr : .word wordvar2
```

Here we can also see the label `wordvar2addr`. We will discuss what this line of code is doing shortly; however, for the moment we are interested in the label itself.

In Assembly language, labels are a way of referencing unique spaces in memory. They should not be confused with directives, which start with a period (such as `.data` and `.text`).

It is also important to remember that the label references the memory address and not the contents. You'll come to have a better understanding of what this means as we look at memory and then addresses next.

The memory

If the CPU has a limited set of storage in the form of registers, then where do we keep larger amounts of data?

This is where the memory comes in. Placing aside the cache and the registers, our Raspberry Pi has two forms of memory. There is the RAM where data is stored as long as the Raspberry Pi is powered.

The second type is the microSD card. This is our long-term storage and memory mechanism. Files are written here and can be accessed again once the device is powered back up.

In our assembler programs, when we want to store data outside of the CPU registers, we tap into the RAM of the computer.

The program contained in the text portion of our program is already loaded into memory when we run it from the command line.

We can define data to be stored in memory as follows:

```
.balign 4
wordvar2:
    .word 3
```

Here we have defined a variable called `wordvar2`. It is 4 byte aligned and is a word length (32bits, which is 4 bytes). The actual value of this variable is the integer `3`.

This could be represented in a binary word as follows:

```
0000 0000 0011
```

The command we can use to load data from memory into a register is as follows:

```
LDR
```

However, we cannot directly load a reference from `wordvar2` into a register. We need to know where `wordvar2` is stored in memory. We can achieve this via addresses.

The addresses

We discussed earlier the code block found at the bottom of the program:

```
wordvar2addr : .word wordvar2
```

Here we have referenced our variable `wordvar2` again, so why couldn't we just have directly referenced that in an `LDR` command?

When we create a variable and assign it a name via a label, we need to know where it is stored in memory, hence the name address. Once we have this address we can then look at it to see where our variable is stored, and the value it contains.

The address is a 32-bit number that can be used to reference any 8-bit portion of memory. For example:

0000 0000 0000 0000

This would be our first byte of memory.

Now let's imagine we have stored a variable at this address. We can take this 32-bit address number and load it into one of our integer registers on the CPU. With this variable now accessible via its address, we can load the value from it.

You may remember when we looked at the C program in *Chapter 2*, *Programming on Raspbian*, we did something similar. Here we defined a variable, but when we actually wanted to assign a value to it, we prefixed it with the & symbol. What you are seeing here is the same concept, the separation between the variable definitions and accessing it to assign or read a value.

LDR and SUB

In this program we introduce you to two new commands, LDR and SUB. You can see them both in the following code block:

```
LDR R2, wordvar2addr
LDR R2, [R2]
SUB R0, R1, R2 @ Subtract 3 from 7
```

The first command we will look at is LDR. This stands for load register. You may be wondering why we have referenced it twice.

In the first instance of LDR we get the address of our variable wordvar2, which is denoted by wordvar2addr. So what we have done is loaded the address of the variable, rather than its value, into the register.

Next, you will see that the R2 register is wrapped in square brackets [R2].

Currently our register has the *address* of our variable, but it does not contain the *value* of the variable.

The square bracket around the second parameter is saying grab the *value* of the memory location addressed in R2 and store the result in R2.

After these two commands have executed, we have the integer value 3 stored in R2.

Finally, we use the SUB command. As you may be able to guess, this subtracts the value in the second register from the first and stores it in register 0.

This block of code demonstrates how we can load a value from memory into a register and then use it to complete a simple subtraction. Our next task is to try the program out.

Running our program

Let's now assemble, link, and run second_assem_prog. We are going to modify our earlier Makefile to include this new program.

Start by opening up the Makefile in your text editor:

```
vim /home/pi/assem_progams/Makefile
```

Update it so that the all statement is renamed second:

```
second: second_assem_prog
```

Following this, add a new section to the Makefile to assemble and link the third program:

```
third: third_assem_prog
third_assem_prog: third_assem_prog.o
                gcc -o $@ $+
third_assem_prog.o: third_assem_prog.s
                as -o $@ $<
```

 When adding spacing to the file, use the *Tab* key in order to align your commands correctly.

This completes the modification of the Makefile. Of course, you could also add the information necessary to compile the Assembly program from *Chapter 2, Programming on Raspbian*, so they are all located in one place.

Your file should look as follows. Remember to use tabs for spacing:

```
second: second_assem_prog

second_assem_prog: second_assem_prog.o
                gcc -o $@ $+
second_assem_prog.o: second_assem_prog.s
                as -o $@ $<
third: third_assem_prog
```

```
third_assem_prog: third_assem_prog.o
                    gcc -o $@ $+
third_assem_prog.o: third_assem_prog.s
                    as -o $@ $<
```

We can now run the `make` command, passing in `third` as a parameter. This will result in our `third_assem_prog` executable being generated:

```
make third
```

You should see the results of the linker and `gcc` displayed on the screen, as follows:

```
as -o third_assem_prog.o third_assem_prog.s
gcc -o third_assem_prog third_assem_prog.o
```

If this step was successful then run the executable:

```
./third_assem_prog.
```

Finally, when you run the `echo` command you should see the result of the subtraction:

```
echo $?
```

The output of this should be the number `4`.

Let's now move onto some more advanced concepts you may be familiar with from other programming languages you have explored in the past.

Adding power to our program – control structures

Within programming languages, control structures are one of the most useful features. They allow us to say things such as the following:

- If this action happens then do this, otherwise do this
- Keep doing this until some condition is met

The most common control structures you may be familiar with are the `if` and `else` statements.

As with C and Python, we can implement a control structure like this in Assembly language.

Also included in control structures are loops. You may have seen these in the format of the for loop and while loop.

The following program demonstrates how we can implement iteration via loops and if else structures in Assembly language via branching.

We will be building upon our previous program where we introduced you to the SUB command, and will also explore some new commands including CMP and BLT.

Create a new file called fourth_assem_prog.s in the assem_programs directory.

To this file we are now going to add the following code:

```
.data
/* Variable definition */
.balign 4
wordvar1:
    .word 30
.balign 4
wordvar2:
    .word 1


.text
/* code definition */
.balign 4
.global main
main:
    LDR R1, wordvar1addr
    LDR R1, [R1]
    LDR R2, wordvar2addr
    LDR R2, [R2]
while:
    CMP R1, #2
    BLT end          @if less than goto end
    SUB R1, R1, R2   @else subtract R1 from R2
    B while
end:
    ADD R0, R1, #1
    BX LR

wordvar1addr : .word wordvar1
wordvar2addr : .word wordvar2
```

Let's now take a look at an example of the ifelse statement equivalent here.

If else statements

There is no specific `if` and `else` syntax available in ARM but there is a way to achieve this using the `CMP` opcode.

CMP stands for compare. It will take the two values passed to it and set a condition register based upon the comparison it performs by simple arithmetic.

In our example program we have specified this as follows:

```
CMP R1, #2
```

This checks the value of register 1 and subtracts the integer 2 from it. If the value is less than 2 after the subtraction, then the condition register records a less than value. Otherwise it will record that it is greater than or equal to.

Following this, we see if the condition register is set to `LT` (less than) using the following code:

```
BLT end
```

If it is less than, we branch to our `end` statement, otherwise we continue with the process of subtracting values until the condition is met.

In the C language we might write this as follows:

```
if ( a < b) {
...
} else {
...
}
```

As you can see, it is fairly easy to mimic this conditional statement using a comparison and branching approach in ARM Assembly language. There are a number of opcodes available for doing other comparisons, such as a greater than.

You can read more about these at the ARM website by visiting `http://infocenter.arm.com/help/index.jsp?topic=/com.arm.doc.kui0100a/armasm_cegihjgh.htm`.

As you may have noticed, we were checking if the value in our program was less than two, and if not, continued subtracting values until this condition was met. This approach used iteration, commonly known as **looping**.

Let's now take a look at this in closer detail.

Iteration

Often when writing a program we want to do a single task multiple times, or continue doing a task until some other event takes place. This is the heart of iteration and is represented by writing loops in programming languages.

You may have heard of `for` and `while` loops, but if not you can read more about the idea behind them here `https://en.wikipedia.org/wiki/For_loop` and `https://en.wikipedia.org/wiki/While_loop`.

So how do we write a loop in Assembly language? Well, in fact we have done that with this very program.

This is the code located in the `while` block:

```
while:
    CMP R1, #2
    BLT end         @if less than goto end
    SUB R1, R1, R2  @else subtract R1 from R2
    B while
```

The process continues to run over and over, subtracting the value of register 2 from register 1. This will only complete when our `if` statement, which is checking if the value of R1 is less than 2, is true. At this point, the loop exits as we call the `end` code.

In C we could represent this as follows:

```
while ( a >= b)  {
...
}
```

Here we are continuing to execute the code in the braces until the variable a is less than b, in which case the program would exit from the while loop.

That concludes our look at control structures; let's see what happens when we run the program.

Testing our control structures

We can modify our earlier `Makefile` to now include this fourth program.

```
fourth: fourth_assem_prog

fourth_assem_prog: fourth_assem_prog.o
                gcc -o $@ $+

fourth_assem_prog.o: fourth_assem_prog.s
                as -o $@ $<
```

Once you have added this to the `Makefile`, save it and execute the following command:

```
make fourth
```

You should now have the executable ready to run. From the command line you can simply type the following command:

```
./fourth
```

When the program has finished, we can check register 0 and see what result is present:

```
echo $?
```

You should now see the value 2. Why 2? After our loop completed, leaving register 1 with the value of 1, we called the end block of code.

In this we added the integer 1 to the value of register 1 and stored it in R0. This resulted in a value of 2 being stored when the application exited.

Summary

This concludes our chapter on the Assembly language, and has provided you with a hands-on guide to programming the CPU and using memory.

The ARM Assembly language is rich with features, and this chapter makes a great jumping off point for those interested in working with the subject further.

Our Raspberry Pi 2, however, contains other hardware components we wish to interact with. As you discovered, Assembly programs can be fairly verbose to write to perform simple tasks, even with the help of mnemonics.

Next, we will return to the C programming language and look at another interesting subject, programming threads.

4
Multithreaded Applications with C/C++

In this chapter we will explore the Raspberry Pi 2 further via the C/C++ languages and a technology known as **threads**.

This chapter builds upon the previous material and will help you to understand how applications can run tasks concurrently. In addition to this, you will see how these concurrent operations can access a shared memory space and manipulate its value without overwriting each other's computations.

Topics also covered include the following:

*   A look at pthreads
*   Writing threaded applications in C
*   Adapting a C-based threaded application for C++
*   Understanding mutexes

To start with we will look at what threads are before writing several applications in both C and C++.

What are threads?

In order to understand threads, it helps to understand what a process is first.

Within Linux, if you run the command ps you will see a list of processes running on the machine:

```
  PID TTY          TIME CMD
20215 pts/0    00:00:00 bash
20231 pts/0    00:00:00 ps
```

A process is a running instance of a program at a particular point in time. We can see in the example that both the `ps` command we typed and the `bash` shell is shown in the list.

Each process has a unique ID identifying it and has a number of other properties. These are:

- System resources
- Security attributes
- Memory
- Processor state

At any point in time multiple processes could be running that need access to the register in the CPU, for example. It is the job of the **short-term scheduler** to decide which process is to be executed.

A thread can be thought of as a sub-division of a process and is the smallest unit a scheduler will work with to allocate resources.

Just as the operating system can have multiple programs running and a program can have multiple processes, a process can have multiple threads.

 A program can be split across multiple processes, which allows the concept of multiprocessing to come into play. This is where a program can leverage more than one CPU to execute itself.

There are of course some differences between threads and processes. A process, for example, does not share its address space with that of another process; however, threads do.

Synchronization between processes is handled by the kernel or in some cases by technologies such as **Message Passing Interface (MPI)**. Thread synchronization is handled within the process.

Within the process, each of these threads is executed asynchronously, and context switching between threads is far faster than between processes. This asynchronous approach allows us to divide our workload up between each thread within a program. As a result of this, a number of benefits can be found. The following example is used to illustrate this.

Take, for instance, a program that is required to process several inputs. These could be values returned from the Raspberry Pi's GPOI pins that take multiple readings, multiple socket connections, or some similar scenario.

If we did not have the option of using threads, the inputs would need to be processed one after another in a sequential fashion. This of course can slow down the program's ability to respond with certain outputs, if, for example, the processing of one input takes longer than expected or the operations needs to wait for another to complete.

In a system that requires real-time input and output this would be very inconvenient, for example, with a web server where multiple users may be trying to access a resource concurrently.

Several different types of thread exist to deal with these issues. Let's take a look at them.

Thread types

There are three types of thread you may see discussed when writing applications. These are as follows:

- User level threads
- Kernel level threads
- Hybrid threads

We will quickly run through each of these types.

User level threads

The first in our list is user level threads. These are created by user level libraries and not by the kernel, thus the kernel has no control over how they are processed.

In user level threads we follow a co-operative multitasking model where the thread is responsible for releasing the CPU when ready, rather than the scheduler assuming this role. This allows fast switching between different threads and thus lowers the overhead.

 You may see references in literature to **fibers**. These are lightweight threads of execution that use a co-operative multitasking model.

Kernel level threads

The next type of thread is kernel level threads. As you may have guessed, these are created and controlled by the kernel itself. There is a corresponding kernel level scheduled entity that maps to the user threads.

Unlike user level threads, kernel level threads implement a preemptive multitasking model. This results in the scheduler preempting a thread in execution and replacing it with a higher priority thread. This methodology therefore allows the scheduler to replace a blocked thread by an unblocked one, thus not holding up the process from executing.

Hybrid threads

Finally, we have hybrid threads, which act as a compromise between the kernel level and user level. In this instance, the threading library is responsible for the process of scheduling, which makes switching between threads very efficient as no system calls are required.

You can read more about these three models at `https://en.wikipedia.org/wiki/ Thread_(computing)#Processes.2C_kernel_threads.2C_user_threads.2C_ and_fibers`.

For a slide-based comparison of the pros and cons of each thread type, check out `http://faculty.cs.tamu.edu/bettati/Courses/410/2014A/Slides/threads. pdf`.

The library we will use in our C programs (`pthreads`) is an interface that generates kernel level threads.

Now let's look at the standard model that this and many thread libraries are built to support: POSIX.

POSIX threads

In Linux, we use POSIX thread libraries. You will see these referenced in C and C++ code with the `pthread` header.

POSIX is a thread execution model that exists independently of the C language. Our pthreads library provides a C interface for interactions with this model.

When we import pthreads we thus have a wide variety of functions available to us. This includes the following:

- Managing threads, including creating and terminating
- Including conditional variables
- Synchronizing between threads
- Implementing mutual exclusion (mutexes)

The documentation for the standard can be acquired via the IEEE standards association website at `http://standards.ieee.org/findstds/standard/1003.1-2008.html`.

Let's look a little further into the steps involved in creating, managing, and terminating threads. We will discuss some of the areas in the bullet points in more detail.

Steps involved in implementing threads

When we want to implement a thread in our program there are several steps to be considered:

- Creation
- Termination
- Synchronization
- Scheduling

We will now look at each of these items and discuss what is involved.

This will give you a high-level overview of the process so you can understand what is happening in the later programs in this chapter.

Links to relevant documentation will also be provided for those interested in reading further.

Creation and termination

The creation step is, as you have probably guessed, the process of generating a new thread. The termination step is the process of killing the thread.

When a thread is generated in Linux it has its own set of register values, a program counter, and its own call stack. It is also allocated memory where the stack is stored. These are used throughout the lifetime of the thread.

A detailed description of the creation process can be found at `http://man7.org/linux/man-pages/man3/pthread_create.3.html`.

Killing a thread involves the inverse of the creation process. In its simplest form the stack is removed and the memory is freed up.

A more detailed description including what happens with regards to mutexes and conditional variables can be found at `http://man7.org/linux/man-pages/man3/pthread_exit.3.html`.

In the C and C++ programs that follow you will see two functions in action that handle the creation and termination phases.

Once we have generated the threads we need to know how to coordinate, we will look at synchronization.

Synchronization

Thread synchronization is an important topic. When a program generates multiple threads we often need to organize them to avoid a number of pitfalls.

There are three key areas we are interested in:

- Mutexes
- Joins
- Conditional variables

A **mutex** is used to prevent multiple threads operating upon the same memory area at the same time. Without implementing mutexes we can encounter problems such as race conditions, inconsistent results, and data loss.

Therefore, a mutex can be implemented to take an asynchronous process and serialize it so that operations take place in a certain order. Thus we can guarantee the program will run consistently each time.

Further information on mutexes can be found at `http://linux.die.net/man/3/pthread_mutex_init`.

Following this are **joins**. These can be used to cause the program to pause until all the threads have finished executing. For example, say we wished to spawn four threads and have each of them estimate pi. We could then wait until each thread has finished executing, collect the results, and then run an average with the combined results.

For those interested you can read more about joins at `http://linux.die.net/man/3/pthread_join`.

Our final category is **conditional variables**. These allow us to perform operations such as halting a program, thus allowing the process to be used for another action until some state is `true`. Conditional variables are used in conjunction with mutexes.

For more information on conditional variables, visit `http://linux.die.net/man/3/pthread_cond_init`.

When multiple threads come into play, a method is needed to say when to execute each one. This is achieved via scheduling. We will let Raspbian handle this, but will briefly explore the concept next.

Scheduling

Raspbian by default will continuously select a single unblocked thread for execution. This default behavior is optimal for the programs we use to demonstrate threading concepts.

Thread scheduling, however, allows a programmer to set the priority of threads and choose which algorithm/policy is used to control thread priority. This in essence allows a program to override the default behavior of the operating system.

The POSIX standard implementation via C allows us to control some details regarding how threads are scheduled. They can be implemented as follows:

- During the creation process
- Dynamically after the creation process
- Via a mutex when creating said mutex
- Through a synchronization operation

Implementation of an override for scheduling is out of the scope of the programs in this book. However, for those of you who are interested, you can read more in *Chapter 4*, *Managing Pthreads*, in an excellent book called *Pthreads*, *O'Reilly*, authored by *Bradford Nichols*, *Dick Buttlar*, and *Jacqueline Proulx Farrell*.

We shall now look at our first example in the C programming language.

In this program we will explore how to generate a number of threads that output text to the screen.

An example in C

Here we have an example C program that implements the thread creation process.

Start by creating a new file under your c_programs folder called second_c_prog.c:

```
vim /home/pi/c_programs/second_c_prog.c
```

Add the following code to this file:

```
#include<stdio.h>
#include<pthread.h>
```

```
pthread_t thread_id[4];

void* thread_processor(void *arg)
{
    pthread_t t_id = pthread_self();

    printf("\n Thread %d processing\n", t_id);

    return NULL;
}

int main(void)
{
    int i = 0;
    int error;

    while(i < 4)
    {
        error = pthread_create(&(thread_id[i]), NULL,
&thread_processor, NULL);
        if (error != 0)
        {
            printf("\nthere was a problem creating thread: %s",
strerror(error));
        }
        else
        {
            printf("\n Thread number %d created.\n", i);
        }
        i++;
    }

    sleep(10);
    return 0;
}
```

Let's now step through what we have here and discuss what it does.

At the top of the file we see we have included two header files:

```
#include<stdio.h>
#include<pthread.h>
```

The first of these, `stdio.h`, you are already familiar with from our first C program.

The second, `pthread.h`, is new. This header stands for POSIX threads and contains the function references we need in order to implement threads in our application.

The next line of code we are interested in is this:

```
pthread_t thread_id[4];
```

Here we are defining an array of length 4. This array by the name of `thread_id` will contain 4 threads.

 The array uses a 0 based index; therefore, the first item is 0, the second is 1, and so on.

Next we come to our first custom function, `thread_processor`:

```
void* thread_processor(void *arg)
{
    pthread_t t_id = pthread_self();

    printf("\n Thread %d processing\n", t_id);

    return NULL;
}
```

The method is responsible for outputting the ID of the thread each time it is called. This is achieved through the `pthread_self()` function. When this is invoked it returns the thread's ID to our `t_id` variable.

Using the `printf()` method we can output this to the screen.

Finally, we exit the function by returning `NULL`.

Following this we define our `main()` function. This is the main entry point into our application. Let's now take a look at some of the lines of code contained in it.

The first two lines are variable definitions:

```
int i = 0;
int error;
```

The integer `i` variable is used as a counter. Each time we create a new thread, at the bottom of the `main` function we increment this variable:

```
i++;
```

Following this is another integer variable called `error`. When we create a new thread it should return a code of `0` to show that no error was thrown. However, if for some reason the thread could not be created, the relevant error code is returned and stored in our variable.

We can therefore check the error variable after an attempt to spawn a thread to see if it was successful.

You may see some parallels here when we created our Assembly language program and returned a number to register `0`. This number could then be viewed via the `echo` command. If our Assembly language program threw an error, this could have been stored in register `0` and when running `echo $?` we could see the exit code that is the error code of the application.

Following this, we include a `while` loop:

```
while(i < 4)
```

This ties into the code that increments the `i` variable. While our variable is less than `4` (starting at `0`) we run the code in the while loop block. Once again, you will be familiar with this idea of a `while` loop from our Assembly language programs.

Now we get to a very interesting piece of code, the thread creation:

```
error = pthread_create(&(thread_id[i]), NULL, &thread_processor,
NULL);
```

As we just mentioned, the output of this is stored in `error`, but let's look at the `pthread_create` function. This function creates a new thread inside of the process, and it takes a number of parameters. The first we have passed in is a reference to the `thread_id` array we specified at the top of the program. Following this, the second parameter is `NULL`.

This second parameter is where we could pass in attributes to the thread creation process. If we leave it `NULL`, as we have, the default attributes will be used.

You can read more about the POSIX thread attributes here `http://man7.org/linux/man-pages/man3/pthread_attr_init.3.html`.

Following this, we are passing in a reference to the `thread_processor` function. This is the code we looked at earlier that displays the ID of the newly spawned thread.

Finally, once again we pass in `NULL`. This final parameter is a `void*` pointer that can point to any user data to be used as input to `start_routine` when the thread starts. Since we have passed in `NULL`, then a `NULL` pointer is used as an input parameter.

[The term pointer is used to describe a variable that contains the memory address of another variable.]

This concludes the call to generate a thread. Following this, we use an `if else` statement to display a message to the screen. If we successfully generated a thread we communicate this; otherwise, we output the error code.

Now we have walked through our program, it's time to try it out.

Trying out our program

We can compile this with `gcc` as follows:

```
gcc -pthread -o second_c_prog second_c_prog.c
```

In this command we have linked the `pthread` library with our own code so we can implement it into the executable file.

Once compiled, you can run the application from the command line:

```
./second_c_prog
```

Something like the following should be output to the screen:

```
Thread 1994273904 processing

Thread number 0 created.

Thread number 1 created.

Thread 1985885296 processing

Thread number 2 created.

Thread 1977496688 processing

Thread number 3 created.

Thread 1969108080 processing
```

To exit from the program you can press *Ctrl+ C*.

Now that we have completed our second C program, let's take a look at how we might write this application in C++.

A C++ equivalent

The following C++ code demonstrates how we can implement the threading program. It shows that there are some subtle differences between C and C++ with regard to outputting strings to the screen. However, as you will discover, C functionality can also be implemented in C++.

It also importantly introduces us to thread termination via the `pthread_exit` function.

As you will encounter C and C++ used heavily in many hardware projects designed for the Raspberry Pi, this program will give you a basic introduction to C++, which you can use as a jumping off point.

You can read more about C++ at `http://www.cplusplus.com/doc/` and find a wealth of tutorials.

Our next task is going to be to create a new file under your `c_programs` directory:

vim first_cpp_prog.cpp

Let's start by adding the `include` statements to the top of the file:

```
#include <iostream>
#include <cstdlib>
#include <pthread.h>
```

Here we include a library to handle input and output, called `iostream`. This provides us with some methods in C++ to handle outputting text to the screen.

Next we include a library called `cstdlib`. This library contains C code that has been ported to work in C++ and contains all the functions that were available in the C `stdlib` library.

You can read more about it at `http://en.cppreference.com/w/cpp/header/cstdlib`.

Following this, we include the header for the POSIX thread library, `pthread.h`.

Now add the following two lines of code to your file below the header definitions:

```
using namespace std;

pthread_t thread_id[4];
```

The first line should be new to you. Here we are saying we want to use the namespace `std`. This allows us to call a function such as `cout` without having to prefix the namespace for example, we can use `cout` rather than `std::cout`.

Following this we have a variable called `thread_id`. You should be familiar with this from our earlier C program, and it serves the same purpose, that is, it saves the thread ID.

Next we are going to add the thread processing function:

```
void* thread_processor(void *thread_id)
{
    long t_id;
    t_id = (long)thread_id;
    cout <<" Thread "<< t_id <<" processing"<< endl;
    pthread_exit(NULL);
}
```

You'll see that this function looks very similar to our C one. The differences are, though, that we are using the C++ method of outputting text to the screen, `cout`.

We also introduce the function:

```
pthread_exit(NULL);
```

This is responsible for terminating the calling thread. Our initial program didn't contain this. You can read more about the thread termination process at http://man7.org/linux/man-pages/man3/pthread_exit.3.html.

Following this, we are going to add the `main()` function of our application. Copy and paste this code just below the thread processing function:

```
int main(void)
{
    int i = 0;
    int error;

    while (i < 4)
    {
        error = pthread_create(&thread_id[i], NULL, &thread_processor,
(void *)i);
        if (error != 0){
            cout <<" there was a problem creating thread: "<< error <<
endl;
        }
        else
        {
```

```
            cout <<" Thread number "<< i <<" created"<< endl;
        }
      i++;
   }
   pthread_exit(NULL);
}
```

You may notice that there are some similarities here with our C program. We have an error variable and an i variable. Both of these are used for our while loop and for recording an error code (or success) when the thread is generated.

When we implement the pthread_create function you'll notice a slight change from before. Instead of passing NULL as the final parameter, we in fact pass the following:

```
(void *)i
```

You may remember that this is where we can pass in user data. In our case we pass in the variable i, which is the counter in the loop. Thus each thread will be assigned an ID based upon which thread it is, that is, thread 1, thread 2, and so on.

As you will see when you run the program, the ID will be a single integer rather than the longer number we had before.

Next we have the if else statement again, and this will display the relevant message based upon the error code.

Finally, we finish the program with another reference to pthread_exit.

Let's compile and run this program and see what the results look like.

The g++ command

We are now going to explore a new command called g++. Like gcc, this is also part of the GNU Compiler Collection.

The g++ compiler is geared towards C++. As you may remember when we wrote our C programs, certain libraries are linked by default. By using g++ we get the C++ equivalent of these. If we used the GCC compiler we would need to specify that we wish to link to the C++ equivalent libraries rather than C. Another interesting difference between the two commands is that gcc will compile to either C or C++; however, g++ will automatically compile our code into C++.

So let's compile and link our program to try this out:

```
g++ -pthread -o first_cpp_prog first_cpp_prog.cpp
```

You will now have an executable output that you can run.

As with your other programs you can run the executable directly from the command line:

```
./first_ccp_prog
```

When it runs you should see something similar to the following:

```
Thread number 0 created
Thread 0 processing
Thread number 1 created
Thread number 2 created
Thread 2 processing
Thread 1 processing
Thread number 3 created
Thread 3 processing
```

You'll notice that you did not need to cancel out of the program. In fact, when it finishes running it returns us to the command line.

Both the C and C++ programs are fairly simple. Next we will explore some of the other concepts explained in this chapter in a more expansive C program that builds upon the earlier one.

Going further – mutexes and joins

We touched upon mutexes and what they are; now we are going to implement a C program that demonstrates how they work.

Create a new file called `third_c_prog.c` inside the `c_programs` directory.

```
vim third_c_prog.c
```

Add the following code to this file:

```c
#include <stdio.h>
#include <stdlib.h>
#include <pthread.h>

pthread_mutex_t mutex1 = PTHREAD_MUTEX_INITIALIZER;
pthread_t thread_id[4];
int counter = 0;
```

```
void *thread_processor()
{
 pthread_mutex_lock( &mutex1 );
 counter++;
 printf(" Counter: %d\n",counter);
 pthread_mutex_unlock( &mutex1 );
}

int main(void)
{

int i = 0;
int error;

  while(i < 4) {

  error = pthread_create(&(thread_id[i]), NULL, &thread_processor,
NULL);
  if (error != 0)
  {
      printf("\nthere was a problem creating thread: %s",
strerror(error));
  }
  else
  {
      printf("\n Thread number %d created.\n", i);
  }
  pthread_join( thread_id[i], NULL);
  i++;
  }

}
```

This program is a variation on the first C program we wrote. However, there are a number of differences. First, we are going to look at the variable definitions at the top of our program:

```
pthread_mutex_t mutex1 = PTHREAD_MUTEX_INITIALIZER;
pthread_t thread_id[4];
int counter = 0;
```

You'll be familiar with the thread_id array. However, there are two new ones, the mutex1 variable and the counter variable.

The mutex1 variable is assigned a value called PTHREAD_MUTEX_INITIALIZER, which can be thought of as a macro that contains predefined values. When we assign this to the mutex1 variable we initialize a mutex with default attributes.

We can then use the mutex in our code to protect shared data from concurrent modifications. That is, we can prevent two threads from attempting to access a variable at the same time, which could result in inconsistent values.

The `counter` variable is going to represent the shared memory space we wish to protect from concurrent modifications. This will make more sense after we examine the `thread_processor` function:

```
void *thread_processor()
{
 pthread_mutex_lock( &mutex1 );
 counter++;
 printf(" Counter: %d\n",counter);
 pthread_mutex_unlock( &mutex1 );
}
```

As we explained, mutexes can be used for preventing data inconsistencies and race conditions. In our function we are going to increment the `counter` variable. There is a risk that multiple threads trying to access the `counter` variable concurrently would result in unexpected results.

For example, one thread may increment the `counter` variable at the same time as another, overwriting its result. In this case, instead of the `counter` variable being incremented sequentially giving us a value of 2, we may find the value overwritten by one thread giving it a value of only 1.

The purpose of this function is to lock the mutex, increment the `counter` variable, output its value, and then unlock the mutex again. Once unlocked, the next threads can then follow the same process to increment the `counter` variable.

We create a lock using the `pthread_mutex_lock( &mutex1 )` function and then remove the lock using `pthread_mutex_unlock( &mutex1 )`.

If we attempt a mutex lock against a mutex currently used by one of the other threads, the thread is blocked until the mutex is unlocked again. Thus we can avoid the issues we discussed earlier.

Finally, in our `main()` function we see another new line of code:

```
    pthread_join( thread_id[i], NULL);
```

The `pthread_join` method is our first implementation of joins, which we discussed previously.

This function call suspends execution until the target thread terminates. In our case we suspend the program until all our target threads (4) have completed.

By applying the mutex and join functionalities to our program we should see a program that generates four threads and increments a shared counter from 1 to 4.

Let's test this and see it in action.

Compile and test

We are going to use gcc to compile this program. At the command line run the following command:

```
gcc -pthread -o third_c_prog third_c_prog.c
```

You should now see a new program called third_c_prog.

You can run this as follows:

```
./third_c_prog
```

The following screenshot demonstrates what the output should look like:

```
andydennis — pi@raspberrypi: ~/c_programs — ssh — 100×34

pi@raspberrypi ~/c_programs $ ./third_c_prog

 Thread number 0 created.
 Counter: 1

 Thread number 1 created.
 Counter: 2

 Thread number 2 created.
 Counter: 3

 Thread number 3 created.
 Counter: 4
pi@raspberrypi ~/c_programs $
```

Here we can see that each thread is created and then the counter variable is incremented. You may notice that the thread uses a 0 based index and the counter variable 0. This is because we initialized the counter variable with the value 0. The first thread, which is thread 0, incremented the counter variable by 1. This differs from the prior examples in the manner in which it addresses thread serialization.

This concludes our final thread program.

A comprehensive guide to threads for those interested in delving further can be found at https://www.cs.cf.ac.uk/Dave/C/node29.html#SECTI ON00291000000000000000.

Now let's recap what we have learned so far.

Summary

This chapter introduced us to the concept of threads. First, we learned what they are and why they are useful. Following this we studied how they can be implemented in both C and C++. This allowed us to apply some of the theoretical concepts in practice. Our programs showed how we can create multiple threads, use mutexes to lock memory locations for concurrent updates, and finally how to terminate threads.

Through studying threads in C and C++ we built upon some of what we have learned in previous chapters.

Next we will look at how we implement a USB HDD as our main storage mechanism rather than use the microSD card. This will allow us to increase the storage capacity of the Raspberry Pi and also learn a little about the Raspberry Pi's boot process.

5
Expanding on Storage Options

In this chapter we will explore how we can expand the storage options of the Raspberry Pi 2 beyond that of the microSD card.

As you come to write more applications or use different media types on your device you may find that the microSD card becomes too restrictive. Also, using the Raspberry Pi with an external HDD allows you to create your own **Network-attached storage (NAS)** device. We will explore the Samba suite of software to achieve this.

In order to use these devices there are some modifications that are required in the boot up process.

We will cover the following topics:

- Setting up the external HDD
- Network attached storage
- Installing Samba
- Testing the NAS for different operating systems

We'll start by looking at the Raspberry Pi and how it boots up, then discuss what changes are required.

Booting up

What follows is a brief explanation of the process that eventually results in Raspbian being loaded. This will provide some context when we come to modify the `cmdline.txt` file in order to boot the operating system from the HDD rather than the microSD card.

Start by running the following `ls` command:

`ls /boot/`

This is the `boot` directory as its name suggests. In here you will see a variety of files that are used in a specific order to boot the Raspberry Pi 2 up into the operating system.

The following screenshot illustrates what this directory typically looks like:

We will now summarize how these files are used in the overall process.

The first step happens when we power up the Raspberry Pi. The CPU and other components start up and the VideoCore GPU kicks off the boot process based upon its firmware located in **Read Only Memory (ROM)**.

This firmware can optionally be updated with the latest version by following the steps in the document available at `https://github.com/Hexxeh/rpi-update`.

For those who are interested, the Raspberry Pi firmware can also be acquired from the repository available at `https://github.com/raspberrypi/firmware`.

 Be careful updating your firmware. Updating to an experimental version can risk locking up your Raspberry Pi. The following guide is worth reading before attempting this task if you are new to it. The *GPU bootloaders* section is of particular interest: `http://elinux.org/RPi_Software`

Next, the `bootcode.bin` file is called. You should be able to see this in the `boot` directory. The `bootcode.bin` file starts the GPU up. While the `bootcode.bin` file is in machine code format, the `config.txt` file (also in the `/boot` directory) is human readable. This can be used to pass configuration parameters during startup.

You can read more about these and `config.txt` at the official Raspberry Pi website, available at `https://www.raspberrypi.org/documentation/configuration/config-txt.md`.

Following this, the next stage is `start.elf`, which is then loaded. `start.elf` is responsible for loading the configuration parameters from `cmdline.txt` and also the operating system kernel (Linux). In essence it kicks off the operating system running on our ARM architecture.

For the tasks in this chapter we are interested in `cmdine.txt`, which we will need to edit once we have our external drive setup.

At a superficial level the boot process is very simple and results in the operating system loaded on the microSD card being used. Since we plan to use an external HDD instead, let's look at getting our hardware setup so we can boot Raspbian from it.

Setting up the external HDD

Next we will explore how we can use an external HDD attached to one of the USB ports to store our programs and operating system. This will involve modifying the boot settings as well as setting up the external hardware.

First of all, we need to know what the disk name of our external hard drive is so we can copy the operating system to it and configure the Raspberry Pi to use it.

The first step is to plug the external hard drive into one of the free USB drives. Once you have done this, you can proceed with the next steps.

Getting the disk name

Grabbing the disk name for the device once it is connected is fairly simple; you'll need this and the microSD card name as we move through this chapter.

Start by loading up the command line if you don't have it open already. There is a utility called `df`, which tells us the amount of space left on the file system of the mounted disk. In addition, it lists the names of the disks attached to the Raspberry Pi 2.

You can run the command with the `-h` flag as follows:

```
df -h
```

As explained, this will list the disks. The following is an example of the type of output you can expect. This will be different based upon the devices connected to your Raspberry Pi:

```
Filesystem     Size  Used Avail Use% Mounted on
rootfs         6.3G  2.5G  3.6G  41% /
/dev/root      6.3G  2.5G  3.6G  41% /
```

devtmpfs	460M	0	460M	0%	/dev
tmpfs	93M	296K	93M	1%	/run
tmpfs	5.0M	0	5.0M	0%	/run/lock
tmpfs	186M	332K	186M	1%	/run/shm
/dev/mmcblk0p5	60M	15M	45M	25%	/boot
/dev/mmcblk0p3	27M	397K	25M	2%	/media/SETTINGS

You will need the disk name of your HDD. As an example this could be as follows:

`/dev/sda1`

 You can use `ls /dev/sd*` to see the drive if it doesn't automatically mount.

In addition to this you will also need the name of your microSD card:

`/dev/mmcblk0p5`

 You can also always find the device name in the `cmdline.txt` file specified as the root value.

Once you have this we can now move onto copying the card's contents to the external disk drive. This will then result in the HDD acting as the new hard drive for the Raspberry Pi and the location where the operating system is loaded.

Setting up the HDD

The process of setting up the external disk drive involves mounting our device so we can copy the microSD card image onto the HDD.

Once complete, our files will be stored on the HDD. However, the Raspberry Pi will continue to boot from the microSD card. Let's now take a look at the steps required to achieve this.

Your HDD should already be plugged in from when you grabbed the disk name. We now need to mount the device to a directory. Create a new directory to be the target of the mounting process:

`mkdir ~/usb`

You can then mount this folder with the following command:

`sudo mount /dev/sda1 ~/usb`

The disk should now be mounted and available to start copying its contents over. Remember, you can use the `df -h` command at any time to see a list of mounted devices.

 To unmount a disk, you can use `umount /disk/name` where `disk/name` is your device.

We are now going to use the `dd` command to achieve this. The `dd` command allows us to convert and copy a file between disks.

We run `dd` from the command line as follows. Remember to use the values from your microSD card and external HDD:

```
sudo dd bs=1M if=/dev/mmcblk0p1 of=/dev/sda1
```

This command can take a little while to run. Let's take a look at what it does.

The first parameter is `bs`. This stands for **block size** and represents the size of the chunks of data copied across. Following this is `if` which is the input to the `dd` command. In our case, this is the microSD card that we are copying the operating system from. Finally, the parameter `of` is included, which is the target device we are copying the data to. This, of course, will be your external HDD.

There are many types of filesystem. A comprehensive introduction can be found on Wikipedia for those interested in reading further: https://en.wikipedia.org/wiki/File_system

Once this process has finished copying, we need to tell the Raspberry Pi 2 to use this to boot the OS in future.

Modifying cmdline.txt

You will remember we looked at the `cmdline.txt` file in the `/boot/` directory. Open this up and you should see something similar to the following example:

```
dwc_otg.lpm_enable=0 console=ttyAMA0,115200 console=tty1 root=/dev/
mmcblk0p6 rootfstype=ext4 elevator=deadline rootwait
```

We can now edit this and update it to include the USB hard disk drive:

```
dwc_otg.lpm_enable=0 console=ttyAMA0,115200
kgdboc=ttyAMA0,115200 console=tty1 root=/dev/sda1
rootfstype=ext4 elevator=deadline rootwait
```

Make sure that /dev/sda1 matches the mount point of your disk. Next, we can repartition the disk.

This process allows us to divide a disk up into smaller units, or merge them into larger ones. You may have seen this on Windows machines, for example, where a single physical hard disk is divided up into multiple drives such as C: and D:.

To repartition a disk in Linux we use the following command:

```
sudo resize2fs /dev/sda1
```

Once this has completed the partition should fill the disk space.

[Remember you can use man resize2fs to learn more about the tool.]

We now need to edit the fstab file. Here we can change the settings so that the Raspberry Pi 2 will mount our new HDD drive on boot up:

```
vim etc/usb/fstab
```

You'll need to add the details for your HDD. The following example assumes the name sda1:

proc	/proc	proc	defaults	0	0
/dev/mmcblk0p1	/boot	vfat	defaults	0	2
/dev/sda1	/ext4	defaults,noatime		0	1

Save these changes to complete the configuration setup. Next, reboot the Raspberry Pi 2. We should now be running from the new HDD.

You can now try adding files to the mounted HDD to see it working.

Network-attached storage (NAS)

Now we have seen how to setup a single external HDD let's take a look at creating a **Network-attached storage (NAS)** device. This is particularly handy if you have a number of machines on your home network, such as Macs or Windows PCs, and want to create a central storage device for files that they can all access.

Setting up the NAS builds up the work we completed in the first part of this chapter.

The technology we will use to achieve this is **Samba**. Samba is an open source application suite that provides both file and print sharing services. It re-implements the SMB/CIF protocol and was originally aimed at Windows users.

You can read more about this at the Samba website by visiting `https://www.samba.org/samba/what_is_samba.html`.

For now, all you need to know is that it will allow you to network your Raspberry Pi 2 and use it as a storage medium on your home network.

Let's start by grabbing the packages we need to set things up.

Installing Samba

We can use `apt-get` to grab the Samba packages and install them onto our device:

```
sudo apt-get install samba samba-common-bin
```

Once the installation process has completed we need to edit the configuration file. This can be found in the `./etc/samba` directory:

```
sudo vim /etc/samba/smb.conf
```

Find and edit the following line:

```
# security = user
```

It should be changed to the following line:

```
security = user
```

What we have done here is remove the comment activating this line in the configuration. If the file does not contain this line you can add it yourself.

We can now add our NAS Samba configuration as follows. Add it to the end of the file, below any other configuration settings:

```
[NAS]
comment = NAS directory
path = /ext4/
valid users = @users
force group = users
create mask = 0660
directory mask = 0771
read only = no
```

The first line [NAS] is the name of the share. You can label this whatever you like.

Following this we have the comment. This is a description text associated with the share. This can be a plain text string explaining what the configuration is for.

After this we include the path. This is the path to our mounted HDD, for example, / ext4/ or /.

Next we include the list of valid users permitted to access the share. Here we use @ users. The next line includes force group. Here we specify the UNIX group name that will be assigned for all users who access the share.

The create mask and directory mask follow on the next two lines. This contains the permissions that all directories on the share are given by default including when they are created.

The final setting read only is set to no. This allows users to add files to the share.

Save the file and exit.

We can now test that the NAS is working.

Testing the NAS

First of all, we will restart the Samba server to pick up our configuration changes.

At the command line, run the following command:

```
sudo /etc/init.d/samba restart
```

Next, connect your user to Samba as follows:

```
sudo smbpasswd -a pi
```

You will be prompted to enter a password for the pi user.

We can now test the network share is working from external devices. Follow the steps in the next section for the device you have. Instructions are included for Mac, Linux, and Windows:

Mac

To connect your Mac to the NAS follow these steps:

1. Select **Go** from the top menu bar and then select **Connect to Server**.

2. In the popup window enter in the IP address of the Raspberry Pi followed by the NAS network folder, for example, smb://10.0.0.64/NAS.

3. Click **Connect** and enter the login credentials.

4. You should now be connected.

This completes the steps to access your Raspberry Pi via the Mac. You can now add and remove files to test everything is working.

Linux

Linux machines can also access the Samba share via the `smbclient` application.

If your device does not already have this installed, you can add it via the following command:

```
sudo apt-get install samba-client
```

Once you have installed it, follow these steps:

1. Start by searching for a list of hosts on your network using `smbclient -L 10.0.0.64` where the IP address is your Raspberry Pi's.

2. You'll now be presented with a list of machines.

3. To connect, use `/usr/bin/smbclient \\\\10.0.0.64\NAS <passwd>` where the IP address is your Raspberry Pi and the `<passwd>` is your password.

4. Once connected you will see a prompt.

The `http://www.tldp.org/HOWTO/SMB-HOWTO-8.html` website provides an in depth guide to using the Samba client on Linux.

This completes the testing of the Samba client in Linux. You should now be able to use the Raspberry Pi 2 for storing files.

Windows

Connecting to the Samba NAS from Windows is relatively straightforward. The following steps illustrate this:

1. Open Explorer up.

2. Select **Network**.

3. You should now see your Raspberry Pi on the network with the name you assigned it.

4. Double click the network folder icon.

5. You'll be prompted for your login credentials.

6. The device will now be accessible inside Explorer like any other.

Try adding and removing files to confirm everything is working.

We now have a working NAS device that we can use to store and share large files across our home network.

Summary

In this chapter we learned how to expand the Raspberry Pi 2's storage options by using an external USB HDD. In the process, we explored how the boot process works and learned some new Linux commands, including dd.

Next, we looked at how we could install Samba to turn our device into a NAS device for saving files from the other machines on our network.

Next, we will look at graphics programming on the Raspberry Pi using C/C++.

6
Low-Level Graphics Programming

So far in this title we have looked at programming in both Assembly language and C/C++. Next we will look at how we can take our C programming skills and explore writing graphics on the Raspberry Pi 2.

This will take advantage of the VideoCore IV GPU. In this chapter you will learn about the following topics:

- The GPU on your Raspberry Pi
- Writing C programs that interact with the frame buffer
- How to draw to the screen via a C program

Let's start with a recap on this GPU unit and some of the technologies it comes equipped with.

VideoCore IV GPU

As we covered in *Chapter 1, Introduction to the Raspberry Pi's Architecture and Setup*, of this title, the Raspberry Pi 2 comes equipped with a Broadcom VideoCore IV GPU.

A GPU is a piece of electronic hardware specifically geared towards calculating complex mathematics and altering memory at high speed for the creation and manipulation of images in a frame buffer.

You will be exploring how to access the frame buffer via a C program shortly.

The graphical processing unit the Raspberry Pi 2 comes with provides a variety of features, including OpenMAX, Open EGL, OpenGL 1.1 and 2.2, and Open VG1.1. We will explore some of these briefly later in this chapter as well.

However, due to the complexity of these technologies, it is out of the scope of this book to delve into each in detail. For those who are interested, a comprehensive guide can be found at `https://jan.newmarch.name/RPi/`, including example programs.

In order to showcase some of the abilities of the GPU you will find a number of example programs bundled with the Raspberry Pi 2 that implement these technologies.

These can be accessed via the `/opt/vc/src/hello_pi` folder in Raspbian.

 If you find the programs on your version of Raspbian are not yet compiled you can use the `rebuild.sh` script to generate the executables.

Let's take a look at these in more detail. You will need to be logged into your Raspberry Pi and have access to the Raspbian desktop.

Sample programs

Your first task is to open a terminal window on the desktop.

Once you have this loaded, navigate via the shell to the `hello_pi` directory:

```
cd /opt/vc/src/hello_pi
```

Each program we will run is located in its own folder in this directory.

We are going to start by looking at some programs that use the OpenMAX API.

OpenMax, an acronym for Open Media Acceleration, is a cross-platform set of C programming interfaces. These are geared towards video, image, and audio processing. You can read more about OpenMax at `https://www.khronos.org/openmax/`.

Let's start by running the first program. This is called `hello_encode`:

```
./hello_encode/hello_encode.bin output
```

We have passed in the name of an output file for the program to write to. If the file does not exist it will be created.

You will now see some text displayed on the screen; the following is a sample of this:

```
Port 200: in 1/1 15360 16 disabled,not pop.,not cont. 160x64 160x64
@1966080 20
Port 200: in 1/1 15360 16 disabled,not pop.,not cont. 640x360 640x360
@1966080 20
```

```
OMX_SetParameter for video_encode:201...
Current Bitrate=1000000
encode to idle...
enabling port buffers for 200...
enabling port buffers for 201...
encode to executing...
looping for buffers...
0 0 0 1 27 64 0 1e ac 2b 40 50 17 fc b0 f 12 26 a0
Writing frame 1/300
0 0 0 1 28 ee 2 5c b0
```

Once `hello_encode` has run you should now see the following file in the directory:

`output`

This is a file in the `H.264` format. `H.264`, also known as MPEG-4 Part 10 AVC, is a commonly used video encoding format. You will find it implemented in a variety of areas, including YouTube, Apple iTunes, and Blu-ray discs.

The following Wikipedia article provides more information on this format:

`https://en.wikipedia.org/wiki/H.264/MPEG-4_AVC`

The output file we generated will be used in a moment as input to one of the other example programs that comes bundled with the Raspberry Pi 2. Let's take a look at how this works.

Navigate to the `hello_video` directory. Let's now try using the output of `hello_encode` as a parameter for the `hello_video` program. As before, this is a binary file we can run from the command line:

`./hello_video/hello_video.bin ../hello_encode/output`

When you run this, you should see a variety of colors scrolling to the top left-hand corner of the screen. You'll no longer be able to see the command line or the Raspberry Pi's desktop.

To exit `hello_video` press *Ctrl + C*. This will close the program and allow you access to the command line again.

By running this we have demonstrated how we can take the output of a video encoding program and then run it on the Raspberry Pi 2.

There is also a demo file in this directory you can try out with the following command if you wish:

`./hello_video/hello_video.bin test.h264`

Once again, press *Ctrl+ C* to exit at any time.

The next example we will look at uses OpenGL ES. This is a subset of the OpenGL graphics rendering suite and is often used for rendering 2D and 3D graphics for computer games.

You can read about the technology at `https://www.khronos.org/opengles/`.

The program is located in the `hello_triangle` directory. Looking in this location you will see a number of other files, such as `Gaudi_128_128.raw`. These `.raw` files are images that are implemented by the `hello_triangle` program.

You can run the OpenGL ES example as follows:

```
./hello_triangle/hello_triangle.bin
```

When the program launches a cube is displayed. This cube rotates and each face contains one of the three raw image files that were included in the directory. To exit, as with our other examples, you can use the *Ctrl + C* command.

Let's look at one more example of this technology in the `hello_triangle2` directory.

We can run this program as follows:

```
./hello_triangle_2/hello_triangle2.bin
```

When this program runs it produces a fractal-style image implementing Mandelbrot sets.

You can exit by pressing the *Ctrl + C* command.

If you look through the `hello_pi` directory you will see plenty more examples you can try out. Also, each directory contains the source code. Feel free to edit it and then use the `Makefile` to rebuild the executable.

This concludes the examples that demonstrate some of the features of the GPU. Let's now take a look at writing applications that directly access the frame buffer and draw color and lines to the screen.

Accessing the frame buffer

When we discussed what the GPU is we mentioned that it manipulates images in the frame buffer.

The **frame buffer,** also known as a **framebuffer** or **framestore**, is a section of the computer's RAM that contains the current video frame to be displayed on the monitor or similar device.

Within Linux, we also have what is known as the Linux framebuffer, which is a software abstraction designed to show graphics on screen via a hardware-independent method.

This can be accessed as a file and its API library can be imported into C programs via the header `linux/fb.h`.

When we open the frame buffer as a file we can then make **input/output control (ioctl)** calls to it. An `ioctl` system call is used to manipulate device-specific I/O operations. You will see `ioctl` calls implemented when interacting with a variety of hardware devices, including DVD drives, USB devices, and similar.

We can use a call to the frame buffer to get the current display settings, for example. Let's take a look at how we can do this.

Check the display settings

Let's write a C program that outputs the value of the display settings via an `ioctl` call to the Linux frame buffer.

Create a new program called `fourth_c_prog.c` in your `c_programs` directory:

vim fourth_c_prog.c

To this file, add the following C code:

```
#include <stdio.h>
#include <fcntl.h>
#include <linux/fb.h>


int main(void)
{
  struct fb_var_screeninfo info;

  int framebuff_filedesc = 0;
  framebuff_filedesc = open("/dev/fb0", O_RDWR);

  if (framebuff_filedesc == -1) {
    printf("Error: Unable to open frame buffer device.\n");
    return(1);
  }

  if (ioctl(framebuff_filedesc, FBIOGET_VSCREENINFO, &info)) {
    printf("Error: Unable to read variable info.\n");
    return(1);
  }
```

```
    printf("Display information: %d x %d, %d bpp\n",
        info.xres, info.yres, info.bits_per_pixel );
    close(framebuff_filedesc);
    return 0;
}
```

We will now walk through the code to understand what is going on.

To start with, we added three headers to the file:

```
#include <stdio.h>
#include <fcntl.h>
#include <linux/fb.h>
```

The `stdio.h` library you should already be familiar with and needs no further explanation. The next two headers are new.

The first is `fcntl.h`. This library provides us with methods for performing operations on file descriptors in Linux.

 A file descriptor is an indicator used to access files and I/O resources. You can read more at Wikipedia: `https://en.wikipedia.org/wiki/File_descriptor#Operations_on_file_descriptors`.

Following this, we then included the `fb.h` library, which gives us methods to access the frame buffer. You can read more about the library at `https://www.kernel.org/doc/Documentation/fb/framebuffer.txt`.

After this we then see our `main()` function.

Here, we defined a `struct` called `info` of the type `fb_var_screeninfo`. This data type is new and this is the first time we have implemented one:

```
struct fb_var_screeninfo info;
```

A `struct`, short for structure, is a complex data type that allows us to combine different data types (`array`, `int`, `char`, and so on) in a nested format within a single block of memory.

The following is an example of a `struct`:

```
struct Example {
    int nums[30];
    char letters[26];
}
```

Here, we have declared `struct` called `Example` that allows us to store both an array of integers and an array of characters.

Data types like this can be very useful for grouping relevant information together.

The `fb_var_screeninfo struct` is used to group together data about the display settings that we can access, such as the bits per pixel. You'll see later in the `main()` function we access this variable and display some of its contents.

Next we need a variable to store our error code in:

```
int framebuff_filedesc = 0;
```

This is like the `error` variable we used in our earlier programs. Here, we have labeled it to indicate it contains the framebuffer file description. We can check the value of this variable at a later stage in our program and display an error message if something goes wrong.

Following the variable definition, we attempt to open the framebuffer and store the result of this operation in `framebuff_filedesc`:

```
framebuff_filedesc = open("/dev/fb0", O_RDWR);
```

As mentioned, we would like to know if we got an error and if so, display this to the user. The following `if` statement checks to see if we successfully opened the framebuffer:

```
if (framebuff_filedesc == -1) {
    printf("Error: Unable to open frame buffer device.\n");
    return(1);
}
```

If it failed, we exit the program and return an error code of `1`.

The next check we perform is to see if we can grab the display settings and store them in our `info` variable. We achieve this by passing a reference to the `info` variable and the call we would like to make (in this case, `FBIOGET_VSCREENINFO`) to a method that handles `ioctl` calls:

```
if (ioctl(framebuff_filedesc, FBIOGET_VSCREENINFO, &info)) {
    printf("Error: Unable to read variable screen info.\n");
    return(1);
}
```

If we cannot successfully glean the data we require, we exit the program returning an error code of `1` and displaying a message to the user.

Hopefully our call has been successful. In this case we now display this information to the screen. Here we show the X and Y resolution and the **bits per pixel (bpp)**:

```
printf("Display information: %d x %d, %d bpp\n",
        info.xres, info.yres, info.bits_per_pixel );
```

The `bpp` tells us the number of bits of data displayed per pixel by the graphics adapter.

Our final calls are to close the file handler referencing the frame buffer and to then exit the program returning an error code of `0`:

```
close(framebuff_filedesc);
return 0;
```

Now that we have a program that pulls data back on the display settings, let's give it a test run.

Testing our C code

As with our other C programs, you can use `gcc` to compile `fourth_prog.c`.

Also, if you wish, you can create a `Makefile`, like we did for the Assembly language applications. If you are using the Geany IDE, this `Makefile` can then be executed directly from the application.

The command to compile our application is as follows:

gcc -o fourth_c_prog fourth_c_prog.c

Once we have our executable we can run it using the following command:

./fourth_assem_prog

You should now see something similar to the following:

Display information: 1776 x 952, 16 bpp

Writing our first program was very simple. Let's get a bit more advanced and take a look at drawing a color on the screen.

Filling the screen with a color

We are now going to demonstrate how to fill the screen with the color red. This seems a fitting color choice since our device is named the Raspberry Pi.

This program starts off looking very similar to our previous one; however, it will introduce you to some new concepts, such as memory mapping, setting, and unmapping.

Start by creating a new program in the `c_programs` directory called `fifth_c_prog.c`:

vim fifth_c_prog.c

We are now ready to start writing our application.

A C program to turn the screen red

Copy and paste the following code into your `fifth_c_prog.c` file.

Once you have done this, we will walk through the code to see what exactly is going on here:

```
#include <stdio.h>
#include <fcntl.h>
#include <linux/fb.h>
#include <sys/mman.h>
#include <string.h>

int main(void)
{
  struct fb_fix_screeninfo info;

  int framebuff_filedesc = 0;
  char *device_map = 0;

  framebuff_filedesc = open("/dev/fb0", O_RDWR);

  if (framebuff_filedesc == -1) {
    printf("Error: Unable to open frame buffer device.\n");
    return(1);
  }


  if (ioctl(framebuff_filedesc, FBIOGET_FSCREENINFO, &info)) {
    printf("Error: Unable to read fixed info.\n");
    return(1);
  }
```

```
device_map = (char*)mmap(0,
              info.smem_len,
              PROT_READ | PROT_WRITE,
              MAP_SHARED,
              framebuff_filedesc, 0);

if ((int)device_map == -1) {
    printf("Error: Failed to mmap to device_map variable.\n");
    return(1);
}

memset(device_map, 0x80, info.smem_len);
munmap(device_map, info.smem_len);
close(framebuff_filedesc);
return 0;
}
```

Let's start by looking at the top of the program and the headers we have included:

```
#include <stdio.h>
#include <fcntl.h>
#include <linux/fb.h>
#include <sys/mman.h>
#include <string.h>
```

The first three we also used in `fourth_c_prog.c` but we have included two more new ones you may not be familiar with.

The first is `sys/mman.h`. This library contains code for memory management. We will be using features from this library including `mmap` and `munmap`. A description of the library's functionality can be found at `http://pubs.opengroup.org/onlinepubs/9699919799/basedefs/sys_mman.h.html`.

Following this is `string.h`, which is used for string manipulation. We need to reference this library so we can include the `memset` function. This is used later in our program to set the screen color.

That wraps up our headers. Let's delve into the `main()` method now and look at some of the similarities and differences with our previous program:

```
struct fb_fix_screeninfo info;
```

Once again we have declared a variable that is of the `struct` type. The main difference to what we declared before, however, is that it uses the `fb_fix_screeninfo` structure rather than the variable equivalent.

`fb_fix_screeninfo` contains device-independent immutable information about the frame buffer. This is in contrast to `fb_var_screeninfo`, which you saw earlier. This contains device independent mutable information about the frame buffer, such as the bits per pixel.

Following this variable definition we declare a further two variables:

```
int framebuff_filedesc = 0;
char *device_map = 0;
```

The first variable is the same as we declared in our program to check the framebuffer. However, we have also included a new variable called `device_map`. This will be used to store the values of the `mmap` function.

Next, we open a connection to the framebuffer and check to see if we were successful:

```
framebuff_filedesc = open("/dev/fb0", O_RDWR);

if (framebuff_filedesc == -1) {
  printf("Error: Unable to open frame buffer device.\n");
  return(1);
}
```

Following this we make an `ioctl` call to assign the `FBIOGET_FSCREENINFO` values to our `info` variable:

```
if (ioctl(framebuff_filedesc, FBIOGET_FSCREENINFO, &info)) {
  printf("Error: Unable to read fixed info.\n");
  return(1);
}
```

As before, if there is an error in attempting to do this, we exit the program.

Our next block of code introduces us to the `mmap` function:

```
device_map = (char*)mmap(0,
             info.smem_len,
             PROT_READ | PROT_WRITE,
             MAP_SHARED,
             framebuff_filedesc, 0);
```

The `mmap` function is used to map or unmap devices or files into memory. You can read a detailed description about the function at `http://man7.org/linux/man-pages/man2/mmap.2.html`.

In our code we pass a number of parameters into the method; in fact, we pass six in total. The first parameter is the starting address for the new mapping. We have passed in the value 0 and the Linux kernel will handle creating this mapping.

Following this we pass in length bytes derived from our info variable. The smem_len attribute is the length of the frame buffer memory.

Next we pass in two values separated by a pipe specifying the memory protection. These are PROT_READ and PROT_WRITE. This means the page can be read and written to. Here, page means a chunk of either virtual or physical memory.

You can check the system's default page size using the following command in the terminal window: getconf PAGESIZE.

Our next parameter is flags. Here we can specify whether updates to a mapping are available to other processes mapping in the same area.

In our case, we pass in the value MAP_SHARED. This means other processes that map this file can see the mappings associated with it.

Mapping a file into memory results in a one-to-one correspondence between an address in memory and a word in the mapped file. This allows the file to be accessed directly through memory.

The final two values we pass in are the framebuffer file description and the offset. In our case the file description is the file we opened earlier using this command:

```
framebuff_filedesc = open("/dev/fb0", O_RDWR);
```

The offset value is set to 0 and thus the length value starts from this position in the framebuff_filedesc file.

After assigning the results of the mmap to device_map we check if there was an error. You will notice that we cast the value of device_map as an integer:

```
if ((int)device_map == -1) {
    printf("Error: Failed to mmap to device_map variable.\n");
    return(1);
}
```

If there was an issue we exit the program, displaying a message to the screen.

Our final block of code consists of the following:

```
memset(device_map, 0x80, info.smem_len);
munmap(device_map, info.smem_len);
close(framebuff_filedesc);
return 0
```

Let's take a look at what exactly is going on here.

You can see we use the `memset()` method from the `String` library to turn the screen red. This is achieved by passing in a number of parameters.

First is the `device_map` variable we just covered. This gives us a reference to the memory space we want to update.

The next value, `0x80`, represents red, the color we fill the screen with. Last of all, we have reused the `info` variable to get the length of the frame buffer.

Directly after `memset` we unmap using the `munmap` function. This deletes the mapping for the address range. You can read more about this function if you wish at `http://linux.die.net/man/2/munmap`.

The last two lines of our application are very simple. The `close(framebuff_filedesc)` function closes the handler to the framebuffer. We then use the `return` statement to exit the program.

Let's try this code out now.

Compile and run the C program

We will once again be using the `gcc` compiler.

The command to compile our application is as follows:

```
gcc -o fifth_c_prog fifth_c_prog.c
```

You do not need to link any libraries. Once we have our program we can run it as follows:

```
./fifth_assem_prog
```

The screen should now fill red, covering up any windows that are open, including the terminal. If you move your mouse around, the desktop will start to re-render, replacing the red.

Here we have seen how to fill the screen with color, but how about drawing a line on it?

Drawing a line

Next, we are going to start drawing to the screen; this is where things get interesting.

The following program demonstrates how to draw a line on the screen. You can then use this as a base to further explore creating new shapes if you wish.

Let's start by creating a new file to store this program in:

```
vim sixth_c_prog.c
```

Plotting pixels and drawing lines

The following code demonstrates how to turn the screen black and draw a line on it. With these two concepts you should be able to go on to create more complex graphics drawing programs. The `line` forms the basis of any shape, such as a triangle or square.

Add the following code to the file you created:

```
#include <stdio.h>
#include <string.h>
#include <fcntl.h>
#include <linux/fb.h>
#include <sys/mman.h>


char *device_map = 0;
struct fb_fix_screeninfo fixed_info;
struct fb_var_screeninfo var_info;

void pixel_plotter(int x, int y, int c)
{
    unsigned int pix_offset = x + y * fixed_info.line_length;
    *((char*)(device_map + pix_offset)) = c;

}


void line_drawer(int x0, int y0, int x1, int y1, int c) {

    int sx, sy, dx, dy, error, error2, complete;

    dx = x1 - x0;
    dx = (dx >= 0) ? dx : -dx;
```

```
    dy = y1 - y0;
    dy = (dy >= 0) ? dy : -dy;


    if (x0 < x1)
    {
        sx = 1;
    }
    else
    {
        sx = -1;
    }

    if (y0 < y1)
    {
        sy = 1;
    }
    else
    {
        sy = -1;
    }

    error = dx - dy;
    complete = 0;

while (!complete)
    {
        pixel_plotter(x0, y0, c);
        if ((x0 == x1) && (y0 == y1))
        {
            complete = 1;
        }
        else
        {
            error2 = 2 * error;
            if (error2 > -dy) {
                error = error - dy;
                x0 = x0 + sx;
            }
            if (error2 < dx) {
                error = error + dx;
                y0 = y0 + sy;
            }
        }
```

```
        }
    }


    int main(void)
    {

        int framebuff_filedesc = 0;

        framebuff_filedesc = open("/dev/fb0", O_RDWR);
        if (framebuff_filedesc == -1)
        {
          printf("Error: Unable to open frame buffer device.\n");
          return(1);
        }

        if (ioctl(framebuff_filedesc, FBIOGET_FSCREENINFO,
    &fixed_info))
        {
          printf("Error: Unable to read fixed info.\n");
          return(1);
        }


        if (ioctl(framebuff_filedesc, FBIOGET_VSCREENINFO, &var_info))
        {
          printf("Error: Unable to read variable info.\n");
          return(1);
        }



        device_map = (char*)mmap(0,
                    fixed_info.smem_len,
                    PROT_READ | PROT_WRITE,
                    MAP_SHARED,
                    framebuff_filedesc, 0);


        if ((int)device_map == -1)
        {
            printf("Error: Failed to mmap to device_map variable.\n");
            return(1);
        }
```

```
memset(device_map, 0x00, fixed_info.smem_len);
line_drawer(0, 0, 100, var_info.yres - 1, 0x80);

munmap(device_map, fixed_info.smem_len);
close(framebuff_filedesc);
return 0;

}
```

Let's now go through this and see what is taking place.

The headers section of the program is the same as the previous application we wrote, so we don't need to revisit this.

However, following the headers we have three variable declarations:

```
char *device_map = 0;
struct fb_fix_screeninfo fixed_info;
struct fb_var_screeninfo var_info;
```

Unlike our previous two applications, these are declared at the global scope rather than at the function level. This is because these variables will be used by more than one function.

As we wish to access both the fixed and variable screen information in this program, we have prefixed the variable name `info` with the type of information it will be storing; for example, `fixed_info` or `var_info`.

Following this, we define a function to plot a pixel on the screen. The pixel is the smallest element we draw:

```
void pixel_plotter(int x, int y, int c)
{
    unsigned int offset = x + y * fixed_info.line_length;
    *((char*)(device_map + offset)) = c;

}
```

This function takes an `x` and `y` coordinate and a color. It then updates the value of the `device_map` variable to reflect this point.

Following this we define a function to draw a line:

```
void line_drawer(int x0, int y0, int x1, int y1, int c) {
```

This is a rather large method and implements Bresenham's line algorithm. You can read more about this on Wikipedia:

`https://en.wikipedia.org/wiki/Bresenham%27s_line_algorithm`

Several implementations of this can also be found in the C programming language for those who are interested. The following site demonstrates the algorithm in C and C++ as well as a variety of other languages:

`http://rosettacode.org/wiki/Bitmap/Bresenham's_line_algorithm#C`

The code in the `main` function will be familiar to you from our previous two programs. In fact it is an amalgamation of them.

Where it does differ, however, is with the inclusion of these two lines:

```
memset(device_map, 0x00, fixed_info.smem_len);
line_drawer(0, 0, 100, var_info.yres - 1, 0x80);
```

This time we fill the screen black rather than red. Once we have done that, we call the function to draw the line on the screen. You can try updating the values here, such as `100`, which represents the x coordinate. Or, if you wish, you could modify the program to take an integer from the command line. This will then reposition the line on the screen.

Our program then wraps up as before:

```
munmap(device_map, fixed_info.smem_len);
close(framebuff_filedesc);
return 0;
```

This completes our line drawing program. Let's try it out.

Compile and run

As before, use `gcc` to compile the application:

`gcc -o sixth_c_prog sixth_c_prog.c`

Once the executable has been output you can run it from the command line:

`./sixth_assem_prog`

The screen will now turn black, and a red line should be present. Where it appears on the screen depends on whether you changed the x or y coordinates.

If you move your mouse around, once again the desktop will re-render.

Next steps – polygons

Now that you can draw a line on the screen, you have the basics for drawing any type of shape both in the 2D and 3D realms.

The following code demonstrates how you might render a square or rectangle on the screen:

```
void rect_square_drawer(int x, int y, int w, int h, int c)
{
    line_drawer(x, y, x + w, y, c); // top line
    line_drawer(x + w, y, x + w, y + h, c); // right line
    line_drawer(x, y + h, x + w, y + h, c); // bottom line
    line_drawer(x, y, x, y + h, c); // left line
}
```

You can try implementing this in `sixth_c_prog.c` and experiment with it.

A term you may come across in reference to graphics is polygon. Polygons form the basis of 3D computer graphics. Traditionally, you will find that many graphics engines use triangles as their base polygon.

It would therefore be fairly simple to take the existing program you have written and the preceding function and update it to render a triangle on the screen in whichever coordinates you wish.

By combining multiple triangles in a mesh it is then possible to render a 3D object. The following Wikipedia article contains some example images that demonstrate this process:

`https://en.wikipedia.org/wiki/Polygon_mesh`

As you explore this feature further you may wish to implement the graphics libraries we discussed earlier, all of which use 3D polygons for rendering. The following guide provides a handy introduction to writing OpenGL-based programs in C++:

`https://open.gl/introduction`

This concludes our look at polygons and graphics; let's recap what we have learned.

Summary

In this chapter we explored some example programs that leverage the power of the Raspberry Pi 2's GPU.

Following this we delved into the framebuffer. Using the C programming language, we wrote a number of applications that used the framebuffer and memory to paint the screen a different color and to render lines upon it.

We ended with a brief discussion on polygons and methods for rendering both 2D and 3D shapes.

In the next chapter we will experiment with the Raspberry Pi's GPIO pins and learn how we can interact with other electronic components connected to our device.

7
Exploring the Raspberry Pi's GPIO Pins

In this chapter we will explore the next piece of the Raspberry Pi's hardware, the GPIO pins.

GPIO stands for **general purpose input/output**. The pins can be used to connect external electronic devices to the Raspberry Pi. This also allows us to build our own circuits and control them using software we have written in languages such as C, Assembly, and Python.

In this chapter we will cover:

- An introduction to the GPIO pins
- Creating simple electronic devices that run off the pins
- Writing Python applications that interact with the pins

We will start by walking through the GPIO pins and looking at what each type is.

Introduction to GPIO pins

The GPIO pins can be divided into a number of categories. These are:

- Standard GPIO
- I2C
- Serial Rx and Tx
- SPI
- PWN and PPM

Let's begin by looking at the standard GPIO pins and understanding what they do. A diagram with a breakdown of the pins can be downloaded from `https://www.raspberrypi.org/documentation/usage/gpio-plus-and-raspi2/images/physical-pin-numbers.png`.

A general overview of the GPIO pins can also be found at the Raspberry Pi website at `https://www.raspberrypi.org/documentation/hardware/raspberrypi/gpio/README.md`.

Standard GPIO

The standard GPIO pins on your Raspberry Pi 2 provide an interface for other electronic devices you may wish to either control or read data from.

These pins can be configured as output or inputs. As you will in see in the Python and C programs we will write, it is possible to programmatically switch between the two.

One important thing to note is the numbering format. There are two different ways in which we can refer to the pins, via the GPIO number or the physical numbering.

The GPIO numbering (also known as **BCM**) is the method by which the Broadcom chip sees them. These numbers will appear to be random to you, so it helps to use a reference sheet.

An updated guide to the numbering format can be found at `http://pinout.xyz/`.

When writing applications, you will need to know these BCM pin numbers in order to switch them between modes.

The second methodology for listing the pins is by their physical position.

You can find the Raspberry Pi 2 physical pin listings at `https://www.raspberrypi.org/documentation/usage/gpio-plus-and-raspi2/images/physical-pin-numbers.png`. This maps the physical pin location to the pin type.

You will also notice from looking at this diagram that a number of the pins are power pins with a specific voltage. These are important to note, and are discussed in more detail later in this chapter.

Let's now look at some of the specialist pins used on the device.

I2C

The I2C standard is used to allow one microchip to talk to another. The Raspberry Pi 2 supports I2C using pins 3 and 5. In *Chapter 10*, *Integrating with Third-Party Microcontrollers*, we explore how to use this methodology to communicate between the Raspberry Pi and a microcontroller.

You can read more about I2C at `https://learn.sparkfun.com/tutorials/i2c`.

With I2C support, we can connect multiple devices to the Raspberry Pi 2 and assign each a unique address. In order to see what devices are hooked up, we can use the `i2c-tool` application.

To install the toolkit, start by running the following command:

```
sudo apt-get install python-smbus
```

This installs a Python module that allows SMBus access via the I2C interface on Raspbian.

A guide to using this module in Python applications can be found at `https://pypi.python.org/pypi/smbus-cffi/0.4.1`.

Once the installation is complete, you can then run `apt-get` to install i2c-tools if this wasn't included when you installed `python-smbus`:

```
sudo apt-get install i2c-tools
```

A guide to the tools can be found at `http://elinux.org/Interfacing_with_I2C_Devices#i2c-tools`.

Let's try checking whether the software installed successfully. Run the `i2cdetect` command with the `-l` flag:

```
i2cdetect -l
```

The command returns a list of installed buses on the Raspberry Pi 2 and for the moment should return no values.

 Remember, you can use `man i2cdetect` to read the manual.

Let's now add kernel support for I2C so we can use it in future if we want. Open up the `modules` file:

```
sudo vim /etc/modules
```

Now edit the file so it looks like the following:

```
# /etc/modules: kernel modules to load at boot time.
#
# This file contains the names of kernel modules that should be loaded
# At boot time, one per line. Lines beginning with "#" are ignored.
# Parameters can be specified after the module name.

snd-bcm2835
i2c-bcm2708
i2c-dev
```

Here we have added these two lines to the bottom of the original file:

```
i2c-bcm2708
i2c-dev
```

Save the file and exit.

 The `raspi-config` provides a GUI for editing the I2C settings as well. You can access this via `sudoraspi-config` and then select the advanced options setting.

Next we need to edit the boot `config.txt` file:

1. Open this up in your text editor:

   `sudo vim /boot/config.txt`

2. Add the following code to the bottom of your file. If you used NOOBS, then add it under the NOOBS autogenerated parameters:

   ```
   dtparam=i2c1=on
   dtparam=i2c_arm=on
   ```

3. We can now reboot the Raspberry Pi so the changes kick in:

   `sudo reboot`

4. Once the device has rebooted you can then log back in.

5. Now let's try the command again. This time, put `sudo` in front; this will show more information when you run the command:

   `sudo i2cdetect -1`

6. You should see something similar to:

   ```
   i2c-1i2c        3f804000.i2c                    I2C adapter
   ```

7. To see any connected devices on the I2C pins, run:

```
sudo i2cdetect -y 1
```

This wraps up the enabling of the I2C port. A huge number of projects are available on the Web that leverage this technology.

The website `https://learn.adafruit.com/adding-a-real-time-clock-to-raspberry-pi` demonstrates how to build a real time clock using I2C support.

Let's now move on and take a look at Rx and Tx pins.

Serial Rx and Tx

The Rx and Tx pins are responsible for **serial communication**. Serial communication is the process of sending data one bit at a time in sequence over a communications medium.

Typically, these ports can be used for console input and output. Thus another serial device can be connected to the Raspberry Pi 2 and the serial data read and displayed to the user, allowing them to debug problems.

This is particularly helpful, for example, during the boot process.

You can see whether the console shell is enabled by running the following command from the terminal window:

```
dmesg | grep tty
```

You should see the following line in the output:

```
[    1.266731] console [ttyAMA0] enabled
```

However, if we wish to use the serial ports to communicate with another serial device such as a modem, then the console login feature would need to be disabled.

This is very simple to do via the `raspi-config` application.

1. Start by launching this:
   ```
   sudo raspi-config.
   ```

2. From the screen that loads, select **Advanced Option**.

3. Then scroll down and select **Serial**.

4. You will be presented with a screen that allows you to switch the login shell on and off.

5. If you wish to disable it select **<Yes>.**

6. Exit from `raspi-config` and then reboot the Raspberry Pi 2.

7. On logging back in via the command line, run:

```
dmesg | grep tty
```

Your serial pins are now available to experiment with serial devices. Later in this book you will experiment with using serial pins to communicate with an Arduino microcontroller.

To learn more about the subject of serial communication, check out `https://learn.sparkfun.com/tutorials/serial-communication`.

SPI

Serial Peripheral Interface (SPI) is a bus designed for synchronous serial communication.

It is useful for communicating between peripheral devices quickly over short distances.

The Raspberry Pi 2 comes with a single SPI bus that has two chip selects. This bus can be interacted with via the SPI pins on the P1 header.

By default, the SPI master drive is disabled, but we can enable it in a similar fashion to switching the Rx/Tx console off via `raspi-config` or by manually editing the `raspi-blacklist.conf` file:

1. To edit via the GUI, start by loading the `raspi-config` command.

```
sudo raspi-config
```

2. Next, select the **Advanced Options** and locate the **SPI** option.

3. From here, follow the options to enable **SPI**.

4. Once you have made these changes, reboot the Raspberry Pi and then log back in.

5. A simple command line test can be run to check everything was enabled correctly:

```
echo -ne "\x01\x02\x03"> /dev/spidev0.0
```

6. If you wish to manually edit the blacklist in order to enable SPI, this can be done via:

```
vim /etc/modporbe.d/raspi-blacklist.conf.
```

7. Here you will need to remove the blacklisting for `spi-bcm2708`.

8. Once this is done you can reload the driver via:

    `sudo modprobe spi-bcm2708.`

A guide to interacting with the SPI bus can be found on the official Raspberry Pi website at at `https://www.raspberrypi.org/documentation/hardware/raspberrypi/spi/README.md`

This link also provides information on the nomenclature used when interacting with SPI.

Later in this chapter, we will install the wiringPi library, which also provides a number of tools for interacting with the GPIO pins, including SPI.

PWM and PPM

Finally, we have a number of standard GPIO pins that can be used for PWM and PPM. PWM stands for **Pulse Width Modulation**. This methodology can be used to control the amount of power sent to an electrical motor, thus controlling its speed. The principle behind this is the implementation of a square wave.

You can read more about PWM and see a diagram of the square wave at `https://en.wikipedia.org/wiki/Pulse-width_modulation`.

It is also possible to generate a software-based PWN square wave using any of the standard GPIO pins. The wiringPi library comes equipped with instructions on how to achieve this at `http://wiringpi.com/reference/software-pwm-library/`. It also includes a number of example projects.

The second acronym, PPM, can also be used to control electrical motors. PPM stands for **Pulse Position Modulation** and is popularly implemented for servos.

Servos — short for servomechanisms — are a type of electrical component, such as a motor, that uses error sensing negative performance to correct its position.

If you wish to undertake any projects that control R/C devices, such as R/C cars and boats, via your Raspberry Pi, this will be of interest to you as they typically implement servos.

You can find a comparison between PPM and PWM at `http://www.endurance-rc.com/ppmtut.php`.

You can find example servo projects at `https://learn.adafruit.com/adafruits-raspberry-pi-lesson-8-using-a-servo-motor/overview`.

Finally, further information and reading on the GPIO pins can be found at https://www.raspberrypi.org/documentation/usage/gpio-plus-and-raspi2/.

Next, we will discuss the power voltages and pins.

GPIO power voltages

With the Raspberry Pi 2, we need to be aware of the voltages used. The GPIO banks all use a voltage of 3.3v. It is important to remember this as applying a voltage higher than this to the pins can seriously damage your device.

The pins can be set to **OFF**, **LOW**, and **HIGH**. You will see this in action when we learn how to switch an LED on and off.

Among the Raspberry Pi GPIO pins, you will also find two 3.3v pins, two 5 volt pins, and several ground pins.

These can be used for powering other devices attached to your Raspberry Pi, either through a breadboard or via the GPIO headers directly.

Hardware choices

There are a multitude of options for connecting devices to the Raspberry Pi. We will touch on a few of these in the following sections. You can purchase these devices if you wish and expand the options that are available for you on the Raspberry Pi.

Regardless of whether you purchase a shield or not, you will need the components listed under the *Connecting directly to the GPIO pins* section if you wish to run the programs in this chapter.

First, we will look at prototyping shields.

Prototyping shields and boards

A number of prototyping shields are available on the market for the Raspberry Pi. A prototyping shield is an electronic component that sits on top of the Raspberry Pi and is connected to the GPIO pins.

Part of the device acts as a breadboard, which allows you to connect a variety of electronic components to it and control them via applications running on Raspbian.

Some examples of prototyping plates include:

- Pi Cobbler
- Adafruit Prototyping Pi Plate Kit
- RKPT Lucia
- Humble Pi

The Pi Cobbler is a popular choice and can be found on the Adafruit website. Unlike the other devices, it does not sit on top of the Raspberry Pi 2, but rather uses a ribbon cable to attach a breadboard to the GPIO pins.

If you would prefer not to use a plate, this is the best option. It can be found at `https://www.adafruit.com/products/914`.

The next shield we will look at is the Adafruit Prototyping Pi Plate Kit. This is a set of components that can be put together into a plate. This plate then sits on top of the Raspberry Pi.

Once assembled, electronic components can then be attached to the plate. This allows you to build a device directly connected to the Raspberry Pi.

The plate can be obtained from Adafruit industries available at `https://www.adafruit.com/products/801`.

A similar device to the Prototyping Pi Plate Kit is the RKPT Lucia available from the RK Education website at `http://www.rkeducation.co.uk/RKPT-lucia.php`.

This kit also requires some soldering to put together.

Finally we come to the Humble Pi. This device can be found at `http://shop.ciseco.co.uk/k001-humble-pi/`.

Once the kit has been built in a similar way to the previous shields, it can be attached on top of the Raspberry Pi 2 and you can then build projects directly on top of it.

Let's now look at an alternative to these types of shield.

Cooking Hacks Arduino bridge shield

The next device we will be looking at allows us to interface with hardware devices designed to work with Arduino.

Arduino is a popular open source microcontroller and will be discussed later in this book when we look at how we can communicate between the Raspberry Pi and other microcontrollers.

A popular feature of Arduino is the many shields that can be attached to it. These shields contain pre-soldered components such as relays, motors, and WiFi support.

You can read more about these on the official Arduino website at https://www. arduino.cc/en/Main/ArduinoShields.

Using the Cooking Hacks Arduino bridge shield, we can connect these third party Arduino shields to the Raspberry Pi.

The following image shows some of the features of the Cooking Hacks shield:

Image courtesy of Cooking Hacks

Using the C++ library provided with the shield's hardware, we can write applications that control the Arduino shields via the Raspberry Pi.

The shield can be purchased from the Cooking Hacks website at https://www. cooking-hacks.com/raspberry-pi-to-arduino-shield-connection-bridge.

Additionally, Arduino shields are available from a variety of manufacturers and stores. A list of over 127 different shields can be found at http://shieldlist.org/.

What if we don't have a shield? Let's look at our final alternative.

Connecting directly to the GPIO pins

Another option is to connect to the GPIO pins directly using wires and a breadboard. In this chapter, we will write programs that use this methodology. You can always adapt these to use one of the other hardware options presented earlier in this chapter.

In this instance you will need a breadboard, wires, and the components you wish to control.

Switching an LED on and off

Our first project is going to be to attach an LED and resistor to the GPIO pins and switch the LED on and off.

We will look at how we can do this using both C and Python. Let's get started setting up the hardware.

Setting up the hardware

In order to build this project you will need the following components:

- LED
- 270 Ohm Resistor
- Breadboard
- Wires

We will setup the circuit as follows; you can refer back to this diagram as needed:

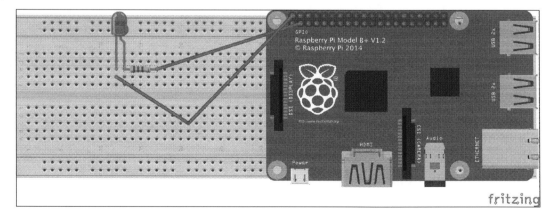

Start by powering down your Raspberry Pi. Next, you will need to attach the wires from the GPIO pins to the breadboard. You will need one from a ground pin and one from a regular GPIO pin, such as number 4.

Next, we need to add the LED and resistor to the breadboard. The resistor is used to prevent the LED from burning out.

These should be configured as per the diagram, so that the GPIO pin wire attaches to the resistor, the resistor is connected to the LED, and finally the LED is connected to the ground pin wire.

Once we have this setup, we are ready to start writing our C program to control it.

C blinking LED program

We will install a library called wiringPi. This is a bunch of C libraries and command line tools that allow us to interact with the GPIO pins.

The wiringPi code can be obtained from `http://wiringpi.com/download-and-install/`.

There are two options for downloading and installing the code. The first is to use Git and the second is to download it as a ZIP, then extract and build the source code.

 Git is a version control system. You can read more about it here: `https://git-scm.com/`.

Instructions for both options are provided at the wiringPi URL. Whichever method you use, remember to install it in the `c_programs` directory.

Once you have obtained and installed the code, you can test it is working by typing the following:

```
gpio -v
```

You should then see the version information output:

```
gpio version: 2.31
Copyright (c) 2012-2015 Gordon Henderson
This is free software with ABSOLUTELY NO WARRANTY.
For details type: gpio -warranty

Raspberry Pi Details:
  Type: Pi 2, Revision: 01, Memory: 1024MB, Maker: Embest
```

```
Device tree is enabled.
* Root or sudo required for GPIO access.
```

We are now going to create a C program that makes the LED we hooked up blink.

Navigate to the `c_programs` directory and create a new file called `seventh_c_prog.c`.

To this file, add the following code:

```c
#include <wiringPi.h>
int main(void)
{
  wiringPiSetup() ;
  pinMode (4, OUTPUT) ;
  for (;;)
  {
    digitalWrite(4, HIGH) ;
    delay(400) ;
    digitalWrite(4, LOW) ;
    delay(400) ;
  }
  return 0 ;
}
```

We will now review the code and discuss what it does.

Let's start by looking at the `include` statement. Here we have included the wiringPi library. This gives us access to a variety of functions we can use for interacting with the GPIO pins, including setting the `pinMode` and writing and reading to/from the pins.

Next, we define out `main()` function. In this, we call the `wiringPiSetup()` function. This sets up the mappings between the wiringPi library and the underlying BCM GPIO pins.

A guide to the mapping can be found on the wiringPi website at `https://projects.drogon.net/raspberry-pi/wiringpi/pins/`.

Next in this function, we set pin 4 to output mode. This allows us to switch a device on and off, such as our LED.

Following this is a `for` loop. This has been defined in a way that makes it run infinitely.

Inside this `for` loop we can see:

```
digitalWrite(4, HIGH) ;
delay(400) ;
digitalWrite(4,  LOW) ;
delay(400) ;
```

Here, the `digitalWrite` function uses `HIGH` and `LOW` to switch between high and low voltage, which causes the LED to blink.

There is a 4-second delay when we do this.

Finally, we return 0 to show no error occurred.

Save and exit this file.

Now we can compile this, including a link to the `wiringPi` library:

```
gcc -l wiringPi -o seventh_c_prog seventh_c_prog.cpp
```

Once compiled, to run the application type:

```
sudo ./seventh_c_prog
```

You should now the see the LED starts blinking. You can press *Ctrl + C* to quit the program. Congratulations, you've written your first program that uses the GPIO pins to interact with other components.

The wiringPi library comes with a number of utilities that can be used from the command line or in other programs. You can read more about these by checking the man page:

```
man gpio
```

We are not restricted to just writing applications in C; we can also use the Python programming language to interact with the GPIO pins.

Python blinking LED program

The following Python program demonstrates how we can turn on an LED as well. As you will see, you do not need to install any third-party software in order to do this.

In the `python_programs` directory, create a new file called `second_python_prog.py`:

```
vim second_python_prog.py
```

To this file, we are going to add the following program:

```
importRPi.GPIO as GPIO
import time

def main():
    GPIO.setmode(GPIO.BCM)
    GPIO.setwarnings(False)
    LED = 4
    GPIO.setup(LED, GPIO.OUT)
    print"Switching LED on"
    GPIO.output(LED, 1)
    time.sleep(4)
    print"Switching LED off"
    GPIO.output(LED, 0)
    GPIO.cleanup()

if __name__ == "__main__":
    main()
```

Let's now take a look at what it does.

To start with, we import two libraries into our program:

```
import RPi.GPIO as GPIO
import time
```

The first is a Python library that allows us to interact with the Raspberry Pi's GPIO pins. You can see we have used the `as` keyword. This allows us to shorten the name of the library every time we reference it. So we can now simply use `GPIO` rather than `RPi_GPIO`.

Next, we import the `time` library. This allows us to use features such as the `sleep()` function, something you will see in a moment.

Following the import statements, we drop in our `main()` function. The next two lines will be new to you:

```
GPIO.setmode(GPIO.BCM)
GPIO.setwarnings(False)
```

We start by setting the GPIO mode. There are two options, board and BCM. These are used to define the numbering method we will use when referencing the pins.

> The following article provides a handy guide to the BCM and board pin modes:
>
> http://raspberrypi.stackexchange.com/questions/12966/what-is-the-difference-between-board-and-bcm-for-gpio-pin-numbering

After this, we disable warnings using the setwarnings() function.

Then, we define the pin the LED is connected to by creating a variable:

```
LED = 4
```

Here we are saying we want to use pin number 4, as we did with the C application.

The next block of code is responsible for making the LED blink:

```
GPIO.setup(LED, GPIO.OUT)

print"Switching LED on"
GPIO.output(LED, 1)

time.sleep(4)

print"Switching LED off"
GPIO.output(LED, 0)
```

We use the time.sleep() function to cause the LED to stay on for 4 seconds, before switching it off with the GPIO.output(LED, 0) function call. You will also note we print text to the screen.

Before exiting our program, we then call the GPIO.cleanup() function. This resets the pins to input mode.

> By default, the GPIO pins on the Raspberry Pi are set to input mode.

Now we have reviewed the code, save the file and exit.

We can test the application by simply running the following:

```
sudo python second_python_prog.py
```

You should see the LED switch on and then off. The following text is also output to the screen:

```
Switching LED on
Switching LED off
```

This wraps up our Python program for interacting with the pins in output mode.

If you want to expand this program, you could experiment with adding a command line option that allows the user to change the speed of the blinks.

Let's quickly take a look at how we can read values from the pins as well.

Reading data from the GPIO pins in Python

The following program demonstrates how we can read data from a GPIO pin. As we currently do not have any hardware connected to the pin, we should expect to see a value of 0 returned.

Create a new file called `third_python_prog.py` in your `python_programs` directory.

To this file, add the following code:

```
import RPi.GPIO as GPIO

def main():

    GPIO.setmode(GPIO.BCM)
    GPIO.setwarnings(False)
    GPIO.setup(11, GPIO.IN)
    printGPIO.input(11)
    GPIO.cleanup()


if __name__ == "__main__":
    main()
```

Here we can see some of the code is very similar to that used for switching the LED on and off.

However, there are a couple of notable differences, which are:

```
GPIO.setup(11, GPIO.IN)
```

Here, the GPIO pin has been set to input mode, using `GPIO.IN` and the following instructions:

```
print GPIO.input(11)
```

In this instance, we print the value being returned from the pin.

Save this file and exit.

We can run this from the command line:

sudo python third_python_prog.py

You should see the value 0 displayed.

The next step is to connect a device such as a button to the GPIO pin. You can then use this to switch the LED on and off.

The official Raspberry Pi website provides a guide on how to do this, and extend this functionality into a reaction game, at `https://www.raspberrypi.org/learning/python-quick-reaction-game/`.

Now you have two options for interacting with the GPIO pins, through C or Python.

You've also seen how you can switch an LED on and off, and how you can read data from a pin. The following list provides some ideas for future projects that combine these two concepts:

- Thermometer
- Parcel sensor using a pressure sensor
- Switching an LED on and off with a button
- Damp sensor

All of these projects can be assembled cheaply using components purchased either online or from a good electronics store.

Let's now review what we have learned in this chapter.

Summary

In this chapter, we walked through the GPIO pins on the Raspberry Pi. We discussed what each of these pin types does and also learned how to enable and interact with them.

A variety of devices that can be connected to the Raspberry Pi were discussed, including prototyping shields and the Cooking Hacks Arduino to Raspberry Pi bridge shield.

We also looked at how this interaction can be facilitated through either a C or Python program. This included downloading the wiringPi library.

These basic skills should leave you in a position to start new interesting projects that allow you to interact with other pieces of electronic hardware.

Next, we will look at exploring sound on the Raspberry Pi 2 through programming.

8

Exploring Sound with the Raspberry Pi 2

In this chapter we will explore generating audio on the Raspberry Pi. This will include:

- Sound on the Raspberry Pi
- Interacting with the GPIO pins
- Writing applications in Python and C
- Generative composition and live coding with Sonic Pi

We will first learn how to configure the Raspberry Pi to switch between either the analogue or digital (HDMI) sound outputs.

Following this, we will discover how we can use the GPIO pins to provide input for playing sounds on the Raspberry Pi via Python. This will introduce us to ALSA. **ALSA** stands for **Advanced Linux Sound Architecture** and provides audio and MIDI support to Raspbian.

After looking at audio via Python, we will then move on to see how ALSA is implemented in C and how programs can be written that incorporate it.

Our final exploration of sound on the Raspberry Pi will lead us to Sonic Pi. You will discover how you can write scripts in the GUI that play a variety of sounds and ultimately allow you to construct your own music.

So let's get started with a brief recap on the Raspberry Pi 2's sound hardware.

Introduction to the Raspberry Pi's sound

There are several options for outputting sound on the Raspberry Pi 2. The first is the HDMI port. If you are using this connected to a HDTV, for example, you can stream both video and audio at the same time.

The second is the analogue audio jack. This is perfect for attaching headphones or speakers that use a headphone-style plug.

However, we are not limited to these two methods.

As explained in *Chapter 1, Introduction to the Raspberry Pi's Architecture and Setup*, the Raspberry Pi 2 implements an **Inter-IC Sound (I2S)** serial bus for both audio input and output.

From the Raspberry Pi's perspective, implementing I2S allows us to not only use HDMI and the analogue audio jack, but also implement audio via the GPIO pins or USB.

We can therefore connect an external device to, say, our GPIO pins that can act as a HiFi system. Later in this chapter we will look at some example hardware that does exactly this.

I2S can be found in a variety of other audio products, including CD players, due to its ability to communicate digital audio data between microchips. You can read more about the specification at `https://en.wikipedia.org/wiki/I%C2%B2S`.

The Raspberry Pi 2 gives us the ability to configure which of our audio outputs we want to use. In this chapter we will build a device that accepts input from the GPIO pins and outputs it to either speakers or headphones connected to the 3.5 mm jack.

Our first task therefore is going to be to understand how we can set the audio output mode.

Configuring the audio output

Before we look at changing any configurations, we will quickly touch upon a command called `Amixer`. This command allows us to control the mixer for ALSA soundcard drivers via the terminal window.

To see what the default settings are, you can simply type:

```
amixer -help
```

This will then display a list of commands.

We are interested in setting the card control contents. This is basically a way for us to switch between using the HDMI audio and the analogue audio options.

The following website provides a guide to `Amixer` and the parameters it accepts:

`http://linux.die.net/man/1/amixer`

Let's now use `Amixer` to set the audio output.

Setting the audio output

To switch the audio to use HDMI, you can use the following command:

```
amixer cset numid=3 2
```

You can switch back to using the using analogue by changing the 2 to 1, for example:

```
amixer cset numid=3 1
```

To revert to the default automatic mode, use 0:

```
amixer cset numid=3 0
```

 You can test the speaker output of the Raspberry Pi using the following command:
```
speaker-test -c2 -t wav
```

The official Raspberry Pi website provides a handy guide to audio setup that you can also refer to at `https://www.raspberrypi.org/documentation/configuration/audio-config.md`.

For the moment, we will leave the Raspberry Pi 2 using the analogue mode. This will set us up ready for our next project. So if you haven't done so, run the command to set the output to analogue:

```
amixer cset numid=3 1
```

Let's move on to the GPIO pins next.

Interacting with audio through GPIO

Now we are going to build upon what we learned in the previous chapter with regards to GPIO pins. We looked very briefly at how we can take a reading from the GPIO pins using Python. However, since we had no hardware connected to the GPIO pin, we got a reading of 0.

The following project involves connecting a number of buttons to the GPIO pins so we can use the input value when pressed to switch between MP3 files.

Before building the hardware, there are a number of software libraries we need to install so we can import them into our program.

So let's start by looking at these.

Installing the audio drivers

We are going to be installing the audio drivers for ALSA onto Raspbian first.

As discussed in the introduction, ALSA is used to provide an audio interface for Linux to the Raspberry Pi's hardware.

The two libraries we will install are `alsa-utils` and `mpg123`.

The `alsa-utils` library contains a number of utilities that are handy for controlling a sound card via Linux. The second library is `mpg123`; this is an MP3 audio player for Linux.

To grab these two libraries, run the following `apt-get` command:

```
sudo apt-get install alsa-utils mpg123
```

Once installed, you will need to power down the Raspberry Pi.

We are now ready to set up the breadboard and electronic components

Hardware setup

We are now going to set up a small electronic device that provides input to the Raspberry PI via its GPIO. Based on this input, we will then choose a drum track to play.

You will need the following components:

- 10k Ohm resistors
- Momentary push buttons
- Breadboard
- Wires
- Headphones or speakers

You can of course user a device such as the Pi Cobbler or a shield to connect the GPIO pins to the breadboard if you wish.

Set up the hardware so the layout looks as follows:

In this diagram, we have the three buttons set up in the middle of the breadboard. In line with these are the 10K Ohm resistors. One leg of the resistor should be placed into the power strip of the breadboard, and the other leg should be aligned with the button.

From each of the buttons, a wire runs into the ground strip on the breadboard.

Finally, we need to connect this to the Raspberry Pi. Run a wire from a ground pin on the GPIO to the breadboard's ground strip where you connected the buttons.

Next, take a wire and connect the 3.3v pin on the GPIO to the power strip on the breadboard where the 10K resistors are connected.

Finally, run a wire from each of the GPIO pins 23, 24, and 25 to connect the resistor and the button.

Once this is complete, we can look at loading the drivers and writing some code.

Loading drivers

Power up your Raspberry Pi, log back in, and reopen the terminal window. We are now going to load the sound drivers. To do this, we will use modprobe, which is a program for adding **loadable kernel modules** (**LKM**) to the Raspbian kernel.

To run this command, type:

```
sudo modprobe snd_bcm2835
```

If this ran successfully, you should see no output on the screen. You can use this command in future, any time you wish to load the sound drivers.

 If you did not switch back to analogue mode, you can do this using the following command: `sudo amixer cset numid=3 1`

Let's now find some audio files to use with the program we are going to write.

Getting some drum tracks

We are going to grab some files to play with the program. Select three drum MP3 samples of your choice from `http://ibeat.org/free-drum-samples/`.

Alternatively, if you have another audio website you prefer to use, grab three files from there.

In the program that follows, we have named these three drum samples `drum1.mp3`, `drum2.mp3`, and `drum3.mp3`. If you choose not to use these names, you will need to change the reference in the code to the MP3 file name.

Python drum machine

Start by creating a new file under the `python_programs` directory called `fourth_python_prog.py`.

Open this file up and add the following Python code:

```
#!/usr/bin/python

import os
import RPi.GPIO as GPIO
import time


def main():
    """ Setup the GPIO pins
        then call the play sound
        method
    """

    GPIO.setmode(GPIO.BCM)
    GPIO.setup(23, GPIO.IN)
    GPIO.setup(24, GPIO.IN)
```

```
        GPIO.setup(25, GPIO.IN)
        play_sound()



    def play_sound():
        """ When the GPIO pins
            receive input we play
            a sound
        """

        while True:
            print "Waiting for input"
            if (GPIO.input(23) == True):
                os.system('mpg123 -q drum1.mp3 &')
            else:
                print "Press button 1 for first drum sample"
            if (GPIO.input(24) == True):
                os.system('mpg123 -q drum2.mp3 &')
            else:
                print "Press button 2 for second drum sample"
            if (GPIO.input(25)== True):
                os.system('mpg123 -q drum3.mp3 &')
            else:
                print "Press button 3 for third drum sample"
            time.sleep(5);

    if __name__ == '__main__':
        main()
```

Now we shall walk through the code to get a better understanding of what the program does.

Let's start with the first four lines of code:

```
#!/usr/bin/python

import os
import RPi.GPIO as GPIO
import time
```

The shebang at the top you will be familiar with. Under this, we have added three `import` statements. You will also remember the `time` and `GPIO` libraries from the previous chapter, but the third library, `os`, is a new one.

The `os` library allows us to run commands from the operating system. Therefore we can use the commands available in this library to call other programs and run bash scripts.

After the `import` statements, comes our first function, `main()`:

```
def main():
    """ Setup the GPIO pins
        then call the play sound
        method
    """

    GPIO.setmode(GPIO.BCM)
    GPIO.setup(23, GPIO.IN)
    GPIO.setup(24, GPIO.IN)
    GPIO.setup(25, GPIO.IN)
    play_sound()
```

Within the `main()` function, we start off by including a multiline comment that explains what the function does. This is also known as a **docstring** and is enclosed in three quotation marks.

Beneath this, we set the GPIO mode and then set three GPIO pins to input mode. Following this, we have a function call to `play_sound()`.

The `play_sound()` function will now be examined:

```
def play_sound():
    """ When the GPIO pins
        receive input we play
        a sound
    """

    while True:
        print "Waiting for input"
        if (GPIO.input(23) == True):
            os.system('mpg123 -q drum1.mp3 &')
        else:
            print "Press button 1 for first drum sample"
        if (GPIO.input(24) == True):
            os.system('mpg123 -q drum2.mp3 &')
        else:
            print "Press button 2 for second drum sample"
        if (GPIO.input(25)== True):
            os.system('mpg123 -q drum3.mp3 &')
        else:
            print "Press button 3 for third drum sample"
        time.sleep(5);
```

After the docstring, we define a `while` loop that runs continuously. Within this loop we check if any of the buttons have been pressed. When they have, we play a sound. If the button is off, we display a message on the screen.

You will see that we use a function call from the `os` library called `system`. This allows us to make calls to the operating system.

Inside the `system` function call, we pass in a reference to the `mpg123` command, which we installed earlier.

For example, we could use `'mpg123 -q drum1.mp3 &'`

In this instance, we call `mpg123` with the `-q` flag (for quiet), an MP3 file to play, and finally the `&` symbol. This will trigger the `mpg123` command to play the MP3 file and run in the background. This will be audible via the device you have plugged into the analogue jack.

The final line of the function creates a 5-second pause. Once this has finished, the `while` loop continues.

Finally, we finish up the program with the familiar `if` statement for kicking off the `main()` function:

```
if __name__ == '__main__':
    main()
```

Save this file and exit. It is now time to try out our hardware and software together.

We can run the application from the command line as follows:

```
sudo python fourth_python_prog.py
```

You should now see the following on the screen:

```
Waiting for input
Press button 1 for guitar
Press button 2 for bass
Press button 3 for drums
```

The program is waiting for input from the GPIO pins. Start by pressing one of your buttons.

You should hear that the corresponding sound plays when the `for` loop starts again after the 5-second pause. One of the messages will also no longer be displayed.

Try each of the buttons and experiment with switching them on and off.

Congratulations, you have now used the GPIO pins to play sound on the Raspberry Pi and build a drum machine.

For further ideas on how to modify this project, you can review the Adafruit *Playing sounds and using buttons with Raspberry Pi* project, which helped to inspire the project we just built and is available at `https://learn.adafruit.com/playing-sounds-and-using-buttons-with-raspberry-pi/bread-board-setup-for-input-buttons`.

Let's now look at some commercial options for expanding the Raspberry Pi's sound capabilities.

Audio shields for the Raspberry Pi

In addition to building our own electronics that interact with the GPIO pins, we can buy off-the-shelf hardware. This includes HiFi and sound card shields. The Raspberry Pi 2 does not come with a built-in sound card, so audiophiles may wish to purchase a more powerful external device.

HiFi shields give us the ability to implement High Fidelity sound via hardware, so we can connect the Raspberry Pi to an AMP or similar audio equipment.

Examples of these devices include the HiFiBerry and Cirrus Logic Audio Card.

You can read more about HiFiBerry at `https://www.hifiberry.com/`.

Further information and purchasing details for the Cirrus device can be found at `https://www.adafruit.com/products/1761`.

Now we have explored audio input and output via the GPIO pins and hardware, let's return to looking at some more software examples.

C and ALSA

In addition to using Python, we can also use the C programming language for writing audio applications that leverage ALSA.

Before we begin to write code, we need to install and compile some C programming libraries.

These are `libasound2` and its development counterpart `libasound2-dev`. Install them using the following command:

```
sudo apt-get install gcc libasound2 libasound2-dev
```

The libasound2 library contains the shared library for the ALSA application. The next library, libasound-dev, is the libasound library's development file counterpart. You will often see –dev versions of packages in Linux, as they contain the headers related to a library's interface.

We are now ready to write our C application. This will check which version of ALSA is installed. The idea behind this program is to introduce you to how to import the necessary library into your program. Once you understand this, you can then implement the example C programs from the ALSA website.

Navigate to the c_programs directory and create a new file called eighth_c_prog.c.

To this file, add the following code:

```
#include <stdio.h>
#include <alsa/asoundlib.h>
#include <alsa/pcm.h>

int main(void) {
  int i =0;

  printf("Checking Audio information...\n");
  printf("Version of ALSA installed: %s\n", SND_LIB_VERSION_STR);
  printf("\nPCM stream types:\n");

  for (i; i <= SND_PCM_STREAM_LAST; i++) {
    printf("%s\n", snd_pcm_stream_name((snd_pcm_stream_t)i));
  }

  return 0;
}
```

Let's now take a look at what is happening.

First, we import a number of libraries:

```
#include <stdio.h>
#include <alsa/asoundlib.h>
#include <alsa/pcm.h>
```

The first include statement brings in the standard I/O library so we can print information to the screen.

Following this, we include the asoundlib.h header file, which we will use to check the ALSA version installed.

Finally, we include the `pcm.h` header, which we will use to display the **Pulse Code Modulation (PCM)** stream types available to us.

You can read more about PCM on the ALSA website at `http://www.alsa-project.org/alsa-doc/alsa-lib/pcm.html`.

Next is the `main()` function. The `int` variable is used later in the program in a `for` loop. The `printf` statement is responsible for outputting text to the screen.

The middle one of the three `printf` statements is particularly interesting. Here we check the version of ALSA installed:

```
printf("Version of ALSA installed: %s\n", SND_LIB_VERSION_STR);
```

This information is defined in the `version.h` file, and in fact this file is imported via the `asoundlib.h` file at the top of our program. The location of `version.h` is:

/usr/include/alsa/version.h

You can open this file directly in your text editor and examine its contents:

vim /usr/include/alsa/version.h

You should see something similar to this:

```
/*
 *  version.h
 */

#define SND_LIB_MAJOR       1 /**< major number of library version */
#define SND_LIB_MINOR       0 /**< minor number of library version */
#define SND_LIB_SUBMINOR    25 /**< subminor number of library version */
#define SND_LIB_EXTRAVER    1000000 /**< extra version number, used mainly for betas */
/** library version */
#define SND_LIB_VERSION     ((SND_LIB_MAJOR<<16)|\
                             (SND_LIB_MINOR<<8)|\
                             SND_LIB_SUBMINOR)
/** library version (string) */
#define SND_LIB_VERSION_STR "1.0.25"
```

The `SND_LIB_VERSION_STR` is the value we output in our program via the `printf` statement. When you run the application shortly, you should see these values match.

Following this, we can see a `for` loop in our program:

```
for (i; i <= SND_PCM_STREAM_LAST; i++) {
  printf("%s\n", snd_pcm_stream_name((snd_pcm_stream_t)i));
}
```

This loops through the available PCM streams and outputs a list to the terminal. You should expect to see PLAYBACK and CAPTURE displayed. PLAYBACK corresponds to outgoing samples and CAPTURE to incoming samples.

Let's now compile and test the program and see these values displayed. From the command line, run the following:

`gcc eighth_c_prog.c -o eighth_c_prog -lasound`

 Remember, you can use a Makefile for your C programs and if you use an IDE such as Geany, run the compiler and similar tools from inside the IDE.

Once compiled, you can run the new program with this:

`./eighth_c_prog`

This will output something similar to the following:

```
Checking Audio information...
Version of ALSA installed: 1.0.25

PCM stream types:
PLAYBACK
CAPTURE
```

Here, we can see the version of ALSA installed and the PCM stream types available, which we discussed briefly previously.

So we have the basics working. Let's take a look at some of the advanced concepts from the ALSA website written in C.

ALSA examples

There are a number of programs you can now run on your Raspberry Pi 2 that come from the ALSA website. These can be found at `http://www.alsa-project.org/alsa-doc/alsa-lib/examples.html`.

We are going to take a look at the program available at `http://www.alsa-project.org/alsa-doc/alsa-lib/_2test_2pcm_min_8c-example.html`.

Copy the code from the preceding URL and add it to your c_program directory.

Before you can run this, you will however need to open it up and make a change. If you try to compile it as pasted from the website, you should expect to see the following error:

```
pcm_min.c:4:34: fatal error: ../include/asoundlib.h: No such file or directory
compilation terminated.
```

The include statement for the asoundlib.h library at the top of the program needs to be modified from this:

```
#include "../include/asoundlib.h"
```

It should be changed to the following:

```
#include <alsa/asoundlib.h>
```

Once you have made this modification, save the file and exit.

It can be compiled as follows; in this instance the program has been named pcm_min.c, but if you named it something different, then update the compilation command to reflect this:

```
gcc pcm_min.c -o pcm_min -lasound
```

This should now compile without an error.

You can run the program via the following command:

```
./pcm_min
```

With your speakers or headphones plugged in, you should hear some random samples.

There are a number of examples on the ALSA website that are interesting to experiment with and provide a base for writing your own audio application.

Before we conclude this chapter, we are going to look at one more audio technology for the Raspberry Pi, called **Sonic Pi**.

Introducing Sonic Pi

Sonic Pi is a free live coding synthesizer, which can be installed onto your Raspberry Pi to create generative compositions. It uses a very simple programming interface to allow you to generate your own sounds and musical pieces.

The official website for the application is `http://sonic-pi.net/`.

An example of the types of sound that can be generated can be found at `http://sonic-pi.net/#examples`.

The very first example at the site generates some bell sounds. The code to generate this is shown here:

```
loop do
  sample :perc_bell, rate: (rrand 0.125, 1.5)
  sleep rrand(0, 2)
end
```

As you can see, the minimal code they implemented on the example site generates some very interesting sounds.

We will now set up Sonic Pi and start experimenting with the programming code to generate all sorts of sounds.

Setup

Raspbian Jessie comes pre-installed with Sonic Pi. If you are using an earlier version of the Raspbian O/S, or find it is not installed, you can acquire it using `apt-get`:

```
sudo apt-get install sonic-pi
```

Once the installation is finished, you are now ready to start experimenting.

Log in to the Raspberry Pi desktop and locate `sonic-pi`. You will need to run this via the graphical desktop as it cannot be run from the command line.

The application can be found under **Start** | **Programming** | **Sonic Pi**.

The desktop application should now load. The following screenshot shows the GUI where you can write your programs:

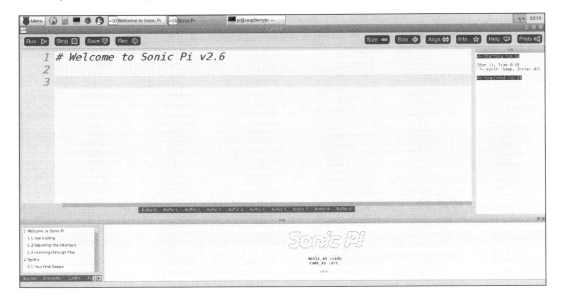

Along the top of the application, there are a number of buttons that can be used to perform tasks such as play and stop the code running in the buffer window.

The Sonic Pi application comes with a tutorial which guides you through the application's menus, function calls, and syntax.

These can be located in the bottom left of the GUI.

Click on the **Tutorial** link and you will find a menu displayed.

In the center of the screen is the buffer window, where we noted our code will be written.

Let's try out a very simple example that illustrates how the menu and buffer window interact. In the buffer window, find the following comment:

```
#Welcome to Sonic Pi v2.6
```

Add the following command under it:

```
play 80
```

Plug in your speakers or headphones if they aren't already, and then press the **Run** button located in the top menu.

You should now hear a note being played. If you wish, try changing the value `80` to another integer such as `83` and press **Run** again. This time you will hear a different sound.

This is one of the most basic applications you can write in Sonic Pi.

Let's now try some more advanced experiments.

Experimenting with Sonic Pi

Starting your first program is very simple, as you saw; you can play a note just by typing `play` followed by an integer.

Let's now take a look at another example like the one at the beginning of this section from the Sonic Pi website.

You may see that in the bottom-left window of the screen there is a list of examples. You can experiment with these to see what the different types of command in Sonic Pi do.

We are going to choose an example called **Pentatonic Beeps** from the Sonic Pi website:

```
with_fx :reverb, mix: 0.2 do
  loop do
    play scale(:Eb2, :major_pentatonic, num_octaves: 3).choose,
release: 0.1, amp: rand
    sleep 0.1
  end
end
```

Paste this code into the buffer window. If you wish, you can select a different buffer tab, such as `Buffer 1`.

This program constructs a simple loop with a pause, which executes continuously. Each time it executes, it plays notes from a major pentatonic scale.

To hear the effect in action, press **Run**.

You should hear the audio playing; it incorporates both scales and chords. To stop it, press the **Stop** button in the top menu.

If you wish to save any of your programs, you can do this using the **Save** button.

Let's try out one more program. This time, we will use the Ocean Waves example as a base. You can grab this either from the website or the examples list in Sonic Pi. The code is also displayed as follows:

```
with_fx :reverb, mix: 0.5 do
  loop do
    s = synth [:bnoise, :cnoise, :gnoise].choose, amp: rrand(0.5,
1.5), attack: rrand(0, 4), sustain: rrand(0, 2), release: rrand(1, 3),
cutoff_slide: rrand(0, 3), cutoff: rrand(60, 80), pan: rrand(-1, 1),
pan_slide: 1, amp: rrand(0.5, 1)
    control s, pan: rrand(-1, 1), cutoff: rrand(60, 115)
    sleep rrand(2, 3)
  end
end
```

Add this to another of the buffer windows and press the **Run** button.

You should hear a sound that reminds you of ocean waves.

This is achieved through combining different types of noise. Let's edit this program to include the sound of a buoy bell. Start by stopping the program.

Add the following two lines above `sleep rrand(2, 3)` in the preceding code:

```
play 80
play 83
```

These two notes will both play in quick succession and sound like they are almost playing together.

Try starting the application again. You should now hear a periodic bell-like chime.

If you want to export this to an external file such as a WAV, so you can play it independently of the Sonic Pi application, this is very simple.

Click the **Rec** button while your program is executing.

A recording will start until you click the **Rec** button again to stop it. You will then be given the option to save the file to your hard disk.

If you wish to save the program, click the **Save** button.

This concludes our introduction to Sonic Pi. You can read more about it using the tutorials mentioned earlier in this section. These will guide you through writing your own advanced projects.

Summary

This concludes our exploration of sound on the Raspberry Pi. In this chapter, we have looked at a number of different technologies for creating sounds on the Raspberry Pi.

First, we built some hardware that interacted with the Raspberry Pi's GPIO pins. In conjunction with this, we wrote a small Python application that took the GPIO input and played an MP3.

We explored ALSA through the C language, and looked at implementing an example from the ALSA website that generated an audio tone.

Finally, we installed and experimented with the Sonic Pi application. Here we saw how simple scripts could be put together to generate music and sounds in a graphical user interface.

Now we will move on to learning more about how we can serve web content via our Raspberry Pi 2. In order to achieve this, we will build a web service using the Python programming language.

We will also examine other options for hosting a web server on our Raspberry Pi.

Building a Web Server

9

In this chapter, we will look at how we can use our Raspberry Pi as a web server. A number of topics are covered in this chapter, including:

- The Hypertext Transport Protocol
- Third party web servers
- Writing Python-based web applications
- Connecting to a SQLite data

We will start by looking at how a web server works and then the third-party software on the market. Following this, we will write a simple web server in Python that displays some HTML content.

Next, we will integrate a small database and display the data. Finally, we will wrap up by looking at what we have learned.

Let's start by reviewing what a web server is and what the Hypertext Transport Protocol that drives traffic to it is.

Introduction to web servers

At its heart, a web server is a system that handles requests via HTTP. You will see the term web server applied in a number of ways, including in reference to the hardware that the software stack runs on, as well as the actual software application itself.

Typically, when visiting a web server you will have data returned to your web browser in the format of HTML, images, JavaScript, and CSS, among other formats. These are what we call web pages, although the web server can also return data in other formats as well, such as **JavaScript Object Notation (JSON)** and **Extensible Markup Language (XML)**.

All of these data types are returned via an HTTP request, which handles transferring the information from the web server to the user's web browser (or another application that wishes to interact with the server).

Let's now look at the HTTP protocol in a little more detail to understand how this works.

HTTP requests

The **Hypertext Transfer Protocol (HTTP)** was invented at CERN (European Organization for Nuclear Research) by the scientist Tim Berners-Lee and his team. Looking for a method to communicate information between physicists, they created the HTML markup language and the HTTP protocol that allows it to be transferred between computers.

An HTTP request can assume one of several methods, the most common being GET and POST. These can be thought of as the mechanism that explains what the request is trying to do.

A guide to these request methods can be found at `https://www.w3.org/Protocols/rfc2616/rfc2616-sec9.html`.

At a high level, the mechanism by which an HTTP request transfer HTML is as follows.

A request is made for a web document via a **Uniform Resource Locator (URL)**, for example `http://www.google.com`. This request also contains more information, such as the version of HTTP being used and the type of request, for example GET.

The web server running on a port accepts the incoming HTTP request and then locates the document on its file system. The document is then returned along with an HTTP header, containing information used by the browser or receiving program. This header includes things such as the error code. If for example the page you requested does not exist, the web server will return a 404 error and a page displaying this error code, along with a message in most instances.

Therefore, a browser requesting a document from our Raspberry Pi will make an HTTP request. The web server installed on the Raspberry Pi will located the HTML document on the Raspbian file system and then return it to the requesting browser.

You can read more about the HTTP protocol at `https://www.w3.org/Protocols/`.

Since HTML is an important component, we will briefly review the subject.

HTML

Hyper Text Markup Language (**HTML**) is the fundamental building block of web content. It acts as a way of marking up documents, so a web browser knows how to render them on the screen.

An HTML document consists of sets of nested tags. These tags represent parts of the document. For example, the header section of the document uses the `<head>` tag and the body of the document, where the main content is rendered, uses the `<body>` tag.

Content contained within these tags can then be styled using CSS (Cascading Style Sheets). These allow us to change the font, color, and other properties of the tag and its contents. While these properties can be changed directly inside a tag in HTML, CSS allows the reuse of sets of properties. These could be styling, such as titles in bold, links in blue, and so on. This helps to ensure the website is consistently rendered and enables easy site-wide changes.

In addition to this, we can then manipulate the HTML tags via programming languages such as JavaScript. This allows us to do such things as finding out which tag (which could be a button) has been clicked on or animating a part of the screen.

An example of an HTML document is as follows:

```
<!DOCTYPE HTML>

<html>
<head>
<title> Hello </title>
</head>
<body id="main">
   <div class="content"> Some content </div>
</body>
</html>
```

This very simple document contains the following components.

The DOCTYPE located at the top of the document denotes that this is an HTML document.

Following this, we have the `<html>` tag. At the bottom of the document is the closing `</html>` tag. All of the content for the webpage is then nested inside these two tags.

After this is the `<head>` tag. The tags located in here are used to provide information about the document. For example, we can include a `<title>` tag. This will not be displayed inside the document itself when rendered by the browser, but will appear as the browser tab title.

Next is the `<body>` tag. This contains all the tags that will be displayed inside the browser tab. In this instance, we have included an `id` for the tag, which is `id="main"`. HTML tags can contain IDs, which can then be used by JavaScript applications to locate and manipulate a tag.

Inside the `<body>` tag we have a `<div>` tag. This division of the screen contains a `class` attribute. A `class` attribute is a way of designating that a set of CSS styles located in a separate file should be assigned to this tag. Our document does not reference a CSS file, however, so no styling would be applied.

You can read more about CSS and discover how to style HTML documents at `http://www.w3schools.com/css/`.

Inside the `<div>` tag we have some plain text. This will be rendered to the browser when the web page is returned from the server.

Each tag in the document has a corresponding closing tag, for example `</div>`.

In the following projects, you will experiment with a simple HTML document like this and return it from the Raspberry Pi's web server.

You can read more about the latest HTML5 standard and its features at `http://www.w3schools.com/html/html5_intro.asp`.

Now we have a basic understanding of HTTP and HTML, we can look at some off-the-shelf open source applications that allow us to serve up content over it. These are, of course, web servers.

Popular web servers available on the Raspberry Pi

Depending on the type of application you wish to serve up, a variety of programs are available to download for free. In this chapter, we will look at two popular open source web servers, Apache and NGINX.

Apache

Apache has been around for a long time and is a well-known web server. You can read about its history at `http://www.apache.org/`.

To install it onto Raspbian we can use `apt-get`. Run the following command:

```
sudo apt-get install apache2 -y
```

This will kick off the installation process.

Once complete, we can test it works by visiting `localhost` in our web browser on the Raspberry Pi or by visiting the IP address of the device from a second computer, for example `http://<ip of rpi>/`.

 If you find the web server is not running, you can use the following command:

`sudo apache2ctl -k start`

By default, an `index.html` page is included with the web server.

To add our own HTML files to Apache, we can place these in:

`/var/www/html`

Rename the existing HTML page to `index.html_old`. You can use the `mv` command for this:

`sudo mv index.html index.html_old`

Next, try adding a new `index.html` file via your text editor:

```
<html>
  <head>
  </head>
  <body>
  Hello Apache.
  </body>
</html>
```

If you refresh your browser you should now see the `Hello Apache` text on the screen.

There are a number of useful commands that can be used for performing tasks such as stopping and restarting the web server.

To stop the web server, run this:

`sudo apache2ctl -k stop`

To start the server up once it has stopped, run this:

`sudo apache2ctl -k start`

For a graceful restart, which will wrap up any existing requests if they exist and then restart the server, you can run this:

```
sudo apache2ctl -k graceful
```

A variety of other commands can be found listed at the following URL, under the reference manual section:

```
https://httpd.apache.org/docs/2.2/en/
```

By default, Apache runs on port 80 of your computer. We are now going to try a different web server, so stop the Apache web server by using the preceding command.

NGINX

A rival to Apache is NGINX (pronounced "engine x"). Like Apache, you can install it on your Raspberry Pi to serve up web content. NGINX is known for its focus on high performance with a low memory footprint. This makes it an especially good choice for a device like the Raspberry Pi 2.

To install NGINX, you can use `apt-get`:

```
sudo apt-get install nginx
```

Once the install has finished, we can start the web server with the following command:

```
sudo /etc/init.d/nginx start
```

Once the web server has started up, we can check the landing page to see it working.

Open up a browser on the Raspberry Pi desktop or a second machine and go to the following URL:

```
http://<ip of rpi>/
```

You should now see the NGINX landing page with the following text:

Welcome to nginx!

As with Apache, we can change this page as follows:

```
<html>
  <head>
  </head>
  <body>
  Hello NGINX.
  </body>
</html>
```

The NGINX `index.html` page is stored in a different location, however:

`/usr/share/nginx/html/index.html`

Try updating this with the new `index.html` file and refreshing your browser.

The following commands can be used for stopping, starting, and reloading the server.

To stop the server, use this:

`sudo nginx -s stop`

To quit, which involves a graceful shutdown, use this:

`sudo nginx -s quit`

To reload a modified configuration file, use this:

`sudo nginx -s reload`

To start the server, run the NGINX executable `sudo nginx`.

More information on the NGINX command line can be found at `https://www.nginx.com/resources/wiki/start/topics/tutorials/commandline/`.

Which web server you choose, if you decide to use a third party one, will come down to a number of things. A good comparison of NGINX and Apache can be found at `https://www.digitalocean.com/community/tutorials/apache-vs-nginx-practical-considerations`.

Now we have seen two third party applications that can be installed on the Raspberry Pi for serving web content. While this is useful, it would be interesting to know how to write our own web server in Python.

This would give us an option for writing lightweight web applications, so we will explore this next.

Building a Python web server

The Python programming language provides us with a number of libraries and frameworks for building robust web applications. This includes the ability to handle incoming HTTP requests, serve up content in a variety of forms including HTML and JSON, and retrieve data from a database and share it with a visitor.

In the first application we will write, we will display the directory structure of the `python_programs` folder.

Start by opening a new file called `fifth_python_prog.py`.

Python web server code

Let's start by adding the following block of code to the file and taking a look at what it does:

```
#!/usr/bin/python

import SimpleHTTPServer
import SocketServer
```

First, we include the shebang, and following this we import two libraries.

The first library is `SimpleHTTPServer`. As you may have guessed from the name, this library provides all the functions and tools necessary for processing and sending HTTP requests and responses.

The next library we include is the `SocketServer` library. This is responsible for providing us with the tools for creating a TCP server, which allows for continuous streams of data between a client machine and a server:

```
def main():
    port = 8080
```

After including out headers we now need to define the `main()` function. The first line we include in this is a variable called `port`. We assign the value `8080` to this. As you will see shortly, this allows us to choose which port on the Raspberry Pi the web server will run on, and can thus be visited by browsers to view our web content:

```
handler = SimpleHTTPServer.SimpleHTTPRequestHandler
httpd = SocketServer.TCPServer(("", port), handler)
print "Serving on port", port
httpd.serve_forever()
```

After defining the port we get to the heart of our web server. To start with, we define a variable that is responsible for handling HTTP requests. Following this, we define the `httpd` variable. This is responsible for creating the TCP server, which will handle the HTTP requests on port `80`.

 TCP stands for Transfer Control Protocol and is usually suffixed with IP (Internet Protocol) to make TCP/IP. TCP is responsible for breaking up data into small chunks, called **packets**, and sending these across the Internet. These packets are then reassembled at the other end. You can read more about TCP/IP here: http://www.w3schools.com/website/web_tcpip.asp

Next, we print a message, saying which port the server is running on, to the console.

Finally, we say we wish the server to run forever, thus accepting multiple HTTP requests:

```
if __name__ == '__main__':
    main()
```

The final line of our program should be familiar to you from our previous Python scripts. Here, once again, we tell the program to call the `main()` function once it has been executed.

Save this program and exit. We can now try running the application. Use the following command:

```
sudo python fifth_python_prog.py
```

You should see the port number that the app is running on displayed on the command line.

Next, from the Raspberry Pi or via a second machine, access the Raspberry Pi on port `8080` in your web browser, for example: `http://localhost:8080/`

A directory listing of the `python_programs` directory should be visible in your browser.

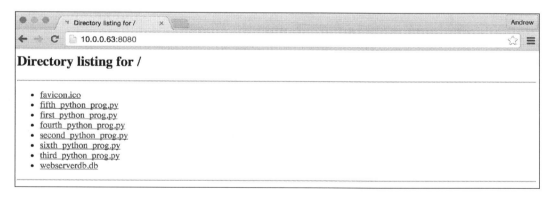

Now take a look at the console window in Linux.

A message saying the application has started on port `8080` should be visible, but also a number of errors:

```
Serving on port 8080
127.0.0.1 - - [11/Jan/2016 09:27:09] "GET / HTTP/1.1" 200 -
127.0.0.1 - - [11/Jan/2016 09:27:09] code 404, message File not found
127.0.0.1 - - [11/Jan/2016 09:27:09] "GET /favicon.ico HTTP/1.1" 404 -
```

These errors are present as there is no `index.html` file and no `favicon.ico` file.

Adding an index page and a favicon

When we first hit the IP address of our Raspberry Pi using NGINX as the web server, we saw a welcome page. We will now look at how we can do the same with our Python web server.

Typically, a web server will list a folder directory (unless this option is disabled) if no `index.html` page is present.

So let's create a simple index page to greet a visitor:

```
<html>
  <head>
  </head>
  <body>
  Hello World.
  </body>
</html>
```

Here we have created a few tags, and in the `body` tag we have the `Hello World.` message.

Save this as `index.html` in the `python_programs` directory.

Once you have done this, restart the web server and navigate back to the URL.

You should now see the following:

Hello World.

We have written an application that serves up a static HTML page and tested it works.

To learn more about HTML, you can follow the tutorials at `http://www.w3schools.com/html/html5_intro.asp`.

Let's now add a favicon. You can use the following website to design your own:

`http://www.favicon.cc/`

Save the file into the `python_programs` directory.

Finally, if you restart the server you should see the error messages have vanished. The favicon should appear on the browser tab. This console can be a useful tool when debugging your web applications in the future.

Adding database support

Rather than having simple static pages like our hello world page, we can display text stored in a database. This allows us to have a page that dynamically updates, depending on the data we have stored.

SQLite

We are going to use a lightweight relational database management system called **SQLite** to demonstrate how our web server can display content stored in a database. We will use SQLite version 3 for this project.

SQLite version 3 can be installed via the following command:

```
sudo apt-get install sqlite3
```

Once installed, you can create a new database by simply specifying a file name after the call to the SQLite shell program:

```
sqlite3 webserverdb.db
```

With SQLite 3, every database is simply a file on the system, so go ahead and run the preceding command. This will now drop you into the SQLite shell. From here, we can use SQL to create a database and populate it with dummy data.

Let's quickly look at some SQL features in order to aid us.

SQL – a quick overview

SQL stands for **Structured Query Language**, and it is used for interacting with an RDBMS (**Relational Database Management System**). It can be used for both the creation of the database and its population and interaction.

Typically, a SQL statement is called a **Query**.

In this chapter, we need to know a handful of commands, which are:

```
CREATE TABLE <tablename>
```

The CREATE TABLE command is used to create a new table in the database.

```
ALTER TABLE
```

The ALTER TABLE statement allows us to edit an existing table.

```
SELECT cols FROM tbl;
```

This statement returns a set of columns from a database table. If you wish to return all of them, you can replace columns with a *.

```
INSERT INTO tbl(col) VALUES (data);
```

We use this command to enter values into the columns of a database table.

```
INNER JOIN tbl1 ON tbl2.col;
```

The INNER JOIN statement allows us to combine the data from two tables and return the result.

You can read more about JOIN, which also provides a Venn diagram for explanation at http://www.sitepoint.com/understanding-sql-joins-mysql-database/.

An in-depth look at SQL is out of the scope of this chapter, but you can read more about SQL and how to use it with SQLite at the following link at https://www.sqlite.org/lang.html. The WHERE and UPDATE statements you will find of particular use.

Let's now write a Python application that implements a SQL database.

Python program with SQLite support

We are going to start by creating a new database to store information on food in our kitchen. You can re-use the one from earlier called webserverdb.db if you wish, or create a new file. Remember, if you create a new file, to use its name going forward where we have used webserverdb.

```
sqlite3 webserverdb.db
```

With the shell now open, run the following:

```
CREATE TABLE storage_location (id INTEGER PRIMARY KEY AUTOINCREMENT,
location VARCHAR(25));
```

This creates a very small, empty table that contains information on kitchen locations where items can be stored. We have named the table storage_location and set a PRIMARY KEY (this is a unique identifier for the record). The key is an integer that increments as each new record is added. Finally, we include a column called location, which can store a 255-character description.

Next, we will add the food_item table:

```
CREATE TABLE food_item (id INTEGER PRIMARY KEY AUTOINCREMENT, location
INTEGER, FOREIGN KEY(location) REFERENCES storage_location(id));
```

This table is used to store a list of food items. Like the storage_location table, it uses an auto-increment integer as the PRIMARY KEY. It also includes a second column. This column is a reference to the location column in the storage_location table. This allows us to mark a food item as being stored in a particular location. In SQL parlance, this is known as a FOREIGN KEY. In order to insert a valid record into this column, it must match a value in the storage_location database. You can think of this as a way of ensuring we don't buy more food than we have places to keep it!

This table is currently missing something though, the description of the food item! So we will now look at implementing the ALTER TABLE statement. This allows us to modify an existing table.

Run the command below in the SQLite shell:

```
ALTER TABLE food_item ADD COLUMN description VARCHAR(40);
```

This statement alters our food_item table to add a new column. This is called description and allows us to store up to 40 characters.

Let's now add a value to our storage_location table. This is going to be Fridge. Execute the following statement:

```
INSERT INTO storage_location (location) VALUES ('Fridge');
```

We can check if this is now in the table by using a SELECT statement:

```
SELECT * FROM storage_location;
```

Here, the * means to return all the columns. You should now see the following results:

```
1|Fridge
```

Let's now add some eggs to the food_item table:

```
INSERT INTO food_item (location, description) VALUES (1, 'eggs');
```

Once again, we can use the SELECT statement to see the item we added:

```
SELECT * FROM food_item;
```

You should now see your eggs returned:

```
1|1|eggs
```

What would be interesting would be to see the location and the item stored in it. We can use the JOIN statement we discussed earlier to achieve this.

Run the following SQL query:

```
SELECT * FROM food_item INNER JOIN storage_location ON food_item.
location;
```

You should now see the eggs and the Fridge returned:

```
1|1|eggs|1|Fridge
```

Here, we have built a simple database that stores information on food items and their location. Feel free to add more items if you wish.

[You can clean up the results to eliminate the IDs from the query by replacing the * with the list of columns you wish to display from each table.]

Our following Python application will now be able to display information from this database, and display it like we did previously using a query, but on a web page.

Flask – displaying database data via Python

We are now going to build a Python web app that connects to our database using the Flask framework.

As you saw earlier, we can write our own simple HTTP server that can return HTML content. As the features we wish to implement grow in complexity, so does our code. Thankfully, a number of frameworks exist that have solved many of the difficult problems for you. By implementing these frameworks, you can cut down on the amount of code you need to write.

The particular framework we will be using is called **Flask**. You can read more about it at http://flask.pocoo.org/.

Flask takes care of setting up the complexities of the web server for us, and allows us to return text from inside a Python program as HTML.

In order to install Flask, we need to install a Python package manager called pip. This tool provides an easy method for installing Python libraries onto our computer, in a similar fashion to how we have been using apt-get.

You can read more about pip here: https://pypi.python.org/pypi/pip.

Start by installing the pip package manager using apt-get:

```
sudo apt-get install python-pip
```

Once this has finished, we can install the Flask package via the `pip` command line tool:

```
sudo pip install flask
```

Next, open a new file in your `python_programs` directory called `sixth_python_prog.py`.

To this file, add the following code:

```
#!/usr/bin/python

from flask import Flask
import sqlite3
```

The first lines of code include the shebang and the `import` statements.

In this instance, we are including the `Flask` framework and `sqlite3`. This will provide us with the tools we need to return data from the database as a webpage:

```
app = Flask(__name__)

@app.route('/')
```

Next, we define a new Flask application and, following this, assign a route. The route is the path you use to access the application after the URL in the browser. In this instance, it is running at the root level:

```
def index():
    conn = sqlite3.connect('webserverdb.db')
    response = ""
```

Following this, we add a new function called `index()`. At the top of this function, we define a connection to our database and also create a new variable called `response`. The `response` variable will store the text to be displayed on the screen:

```
    cursor = conn.execute("SELECT * FROM food_item INNER JOIN storage_
    location ON food_item.location")
```

The next line of code involves creating a variable called `cursor`, which contains our SQL query inside of a function. You will notice this is the query we used earlier that performed the `JOIN`. The SQL query is executed by the `conn.execute` function, and the results are stored in the cursor variable:

```
    for row in cursor:
        response = response + "<strong>Food</strong> = " + str(row[2])
 + "<br />"
        response = response + "<strong>Location</strong> = " +
str(row[4]) + "<br />"
    conn.close()
```

Following the execution of our query, we loop through the results and extract the data we are interested in. This is the location and the food items. These are stored in the response variable as a string, with some HTML tags to help formatting.

 You can also modify the query to only return the columns you wish, by replacing the * with the column name.

Next, we close the database connection we opened:

```
return response
```

The final line of our function returns the `response` variable so it can be output to the browser. The visitor should expect to see a list of items and locations when they visit the page.

```
if __name__ == '__main__':
    app.run(debug=True, host='0.0.0.0')
```

Finally we include some code that starts up the application when the script is run. This tells the Flask application to run on the localhost of our Raspberry Pi 2 and to run in debug mode.

Now we can test our application from the command line:

```
sudo python sixth_python_prog.py
```

Navigate to the IP address of your Raspberry Pi or localhost if you are on its desktop. The application will be running on port 5000 by default.

You should see the following:

```
Food = eggs
```

```
Location = Fridge
```

Congratulations, you now having a working web application that displays data from inside a SQLite database.

Next steps

This project can easily be expanded to allow the user to enter data into the database via a web form.

A handy guide for building web forms using Flask can be found at `https://pythonspot.com/flask-web-forms/`.

Using the earlier example program, you should be able to modify it to use the INSERT INTO statement. Combining this with a web form will allow a web-based method for updating the database's contents.

Summary

In this chapter, we learned a little about HTTP. We came to understand how it could be used for serving up content over the Internet. Next, we studied web servers and how they can be used as the mechanism for serving this content to the browser, in order to be rendered with HTML.

Following this, we used our Python skills, developed in earlier chapters, to write a couple of web servers. The first served a simple HTML page, and the second pulled data from a SQLite database and implemented the Flask framework.

This now leads us to our final chapter on connecting to third party microcontrollers. Here we will look at how other devices such as Arduino can talk to the Raspberry Pi.

10
Integrating with Third-Party Microcontrollers

In this chapter, we will explore how we can integrate third-party microcontrollers into a project using the Raspberry Pi. This allows us to then build a variety of projects, from home automation to robotics. Here, we will bring together some of the skills we have learned over the previous chapters. In this chapter we will cover the following topics:

- The Genuino/Arduino microcontroller
- Setting up the Arduino software
- Working with the serial and I2C pins we enabled earlier in the book
- Communicating between devices using Python and the Arduino programming language

For the projects in this chapter you will need the following components:

- Genuino/Arduino Uno
- USB cable
- 1.6 and 3.3 Ohm resistors
- Wires and breadboard
- Ethernet shield (optional if you wish to try out the Arduino web server examples)

We have chosen the Ardunio Uno microcontroller as it is popular, cheap and versatile. Next, we will look at it in more detail.

Genuino/Arduino microcontroller

Genuino/Arduino is a range of open source microcontrollers developed by Massimo Banzi in Italy during the early 2000s. They have been geared toward students and the open source hardware hacking community. With products ranging from wearable microcontrollers to the wireless Arduino Yun, the range of projects available to enthusiasts is only limited by the imagination.

In the US, the product is branded with the Arduino name. Outside of the US you will see the Genuino branding. This is due to an ongoing legal dispute over the copyright outside of the US. You can read more about this at `http://makezine.com/2015/05/16/arduino-adafruit-manufacturing-genuino/`.

The full range of boards can be found at the official Arduino website at `https://www.arduino.cc/en/Main/GenuinoBrand`.

Software developed for Arduino is done via a free programming development environment. The Arduino sketch programming language was based upon the open source Wiring platform. You can read more about this at the Wiring website at `http://wiring.org.co/`.

Typically, Arduino boards are made up of a microcontroller chip along with a number of other features, including GPIO pins and USB ports.

We are going to be using the Arduino/Genuino Uno as well as an Uno-compatible Ethernet Shield. The following image demonstrates the layout of the board:

A complete guide to the device and its microcontroller chipset can be found at the `arduino.cc` website:

```
https://www.arduino.cc/en/Main/ArduinoBoardUno
```

Looking at the image, you can see there are a number of GPIO headers located on both the top and bottom of the board. These give us access to the power pins and data pins. The data pins are both analog (six total) and digital. The board also contains a reset switch, an ISCP header, a power connector and a USB port. For the power you will need an AC-to-DC power adapter. When the device is plugged into a computer via USB, it can draw power through the USB cable.

Let's now take a look at the software you need to install to program the Uno.

Setting up the Arduino software

Our first task will be to install a copy of the Arduino **IDE** (Integrated Development Environment) on our Raspberry Pi. The Arduino IDE is where we will write sketches—these are Arduino programs. The IDE also allows us to upload the code directly to the Arduino Uno.

The software can be found at the official Arduino website: `http://arduino.cc/en/main/software`

The installation instructions cover a variety of operating systems, including Linux, Mac OSX, and Windows. For the Raspberry Pi you will want the Linux instructions.

You can, of course, install the IDE onto a separate computer and use this for updating the Arduino if you wish.

The following section will provide a quick overview of the Linux installation process.

Installing the IDE on your Raspberry Pi 2

To install the IDE directly onto your Raspberry Pi 2, you can use the terminal.

1. Open a new command line, or via your SSH connection run the following command:

   ```
   sudo apt-get install arduino
   ```

2. Accept any prompts displayed on the screen.

3. When the installation is complete you will be able to open the IDE on your Raspberry Pi. You can access it from the desktop and connect your Arduino Uno directly to the USB drive.

Currently, version 1.0 of the IDE is installed. Depending on whether you run the IDE from your Raspberry Pi 2 or another computer, you may see some slight differences in the menu structure mainly around the Arduino/Genuino naming convention.

A quick guide to the Arduino IDE

The Arduino IDE is a graphical user interface that allows you to develop an Arduino sketch and then upload it to the microcontroller via a USB cable.

1. When you opened the IDE you will have been presented with an empty sketch. This is where we will add code for our projects.

2. Located at the top of the IDE, you will find a number of menu items. Included are a number of out-of-the-box examples. These can be found under **File | Examples**.

3. Select the option **0.1 Basics | Bare Minimum**.

4. This will load a very simple example Arduino sketch. In fact, you will notice it looks the same as the default sketch created when you open the Arduino IDE, if using a later version of the software. Earlier versions normally have just a blank sketch so this may be new to you:

```
void setup() {
  // put your setup code here, to run once:

}

void loop() {
  // put your main code here, to run repeatedly:

}
```

5. Upload this example to your Arduino Uno. Next, you will need to set the board type. You can do this by selecting **Tools | Board**.

6. Here you will find a list of Arduino microcontrollers and you can select **Arduino | Genuino Uno**. Next, we need to select the USB port that we plugged our microcontroller into. This is so the Arduino IDE can upload the sketch code. You can access the USB port from the **Tools** menu: **Tools | Serial Port**.

7. Once you have the USB correctly selected, we can upload the code.

This is done via the play button icon on the sketch. If everything was configured correctly your code should now be running on the Uno.

Before you start the next steps, make sure to unplug the Arduino from the USB port.

Integration with Arduino

As you may remember, we enabled the serial port on the Raspberry Pi earlier. We are now going to install a Python library called **PySerial** that allows us to communicate via Python.

This can be installed via `apt-get`:

```
sudo apt-get install python-serial
```

 If you already have the latest version of the library, you will see this message:

```
python-serial is already the newest version.
```

Once you have this installed you can read more about the library at the PySerial website: `https://pythonhosted.org/pyserial/`.

Before we start writing applications with PySerial, we need to know where our Arduino is connected. You may have noticed that this information was provided in the Arduino IDE when you selected the serial port. If you used a different machine to write the sketch, however, there is a method we can use to find out where it is plugged in.

Start by running the following command:

```
ls /dev/tty*
```

This will output a list to your screen. Currently, the Arduino Uno isn't connected, so make a list of everything you see here. You can use the following command:

```
ls /dev/tty* | cat >> devices.txt
```

This will create a text document, which you will use momentarily.

Serial communication over USB

We can use the list we generated to now find where our Arduino is connected via USB. Start by plugging the Uno into the USB drive.

If you now run `ls /dev/tty*`, you should see the list has changed since you last looked at it to include the Arduino.

We can confirm this as follows. Generate a second list:

```
ls /dev/tty* | cat >> new_devices.txt
```

We can use the `diff` command to compare the two lists and see the differences:

```
diff new_devices.txt devices.txt
```

The difference between the two lists should reflect the Uno connected via the USB port.

Make a note of this value as we will be using it in our program.

Let's start by writing a sketch for the Arduino Uno. We are going to send a message to the Raspberry Pi that says `Ping`. The Raspberry Pi will then output this to the command line.

Open a new sketch and add the following code:

```
void setup(){
  Serial.begin(9600);
}
void loop(){
  Serial.println("Ping");
  delay(3000);
  if (Serial.available()) {
    Serial.print(Serial.read());
  }

}
```

Let's walk through what the code is doing:

```
void setup(){
  Serial.begin(9600);
}
```

Every Arduino sketch has a setup function, which is run first. In this instance we have set the Arduino to use a data transfer rate of `9600` bits per second. This is sometimes known as the **baud** rate.

Following this we declared our loop function. This will run continuously:

```
Serial.println("Ping");
delay(3000);
```

The first line here prints out to the serial connection the word `Ping`. Following this we have a delay of 3 seconds.

```
if (Serial.available()) {
  print(Serial.read());
}
```

Next we check to see if `Serial` is available, and if it is we print out any data we read.

Save this file as `first_arduino_sketch` and upload it via the USB drive to your Arduino Uno.

Next, we will write some Python code that accepts an incoming request via the `serial` port.

Create a new file in your `python_programs` directory called `eighth_python_prog.py`.

To this file add, the following code:

```
#!/usr/bin/python
import serial

def main():
    input = serial.Serial('/dev/ttyACM0', 9600)
    while 1 :
        text = input.readline()
        print text

if __name__ == '__main__':
    main()
```

Let's take a look at what exactly is going on here:

```
import serial
```

First we import the serial library. This is PySerial, which we installed earlier.

Following this, we define our main function and include a number of lines of code:

```
    input = serial.Serial('/dev/ttyACM0', 9600)
    while 1 :
        text = input.readline()
        print text
```

The first stores a connection to the serial port we located earlier. You will need to replace `ttyACM0` with the value you grabbed from running `diff`.

Following this we have a `while` loop that runs infinitely.

Inside this loop we read any incoming serial data and then write it to a variable, which we print to the screen. It's a fairly simple script, so let's try it out.

Save the file and exit.

To run it, use the following command:

```
python eighth_python_prog.py
```

Next, open the **Serial Monitor** from the Arduino IDE tool bar. This can be found under **Tools | Serial Monitor**.

With the two applications running now, you should see the `Ping` message being transferred between devices.

On the command line you will see the following:

```
Ping
```

With the basics in place, you can then modify the script to send more data, send different types of data, or send a response from the Raspberry Pi back to the Arduino.

Let's now look at how we can instead use the GPIO pins to communicate with the Arduino. This allows us to then free up the USB port on the Uno.

Communication between the Arduino and Raspberry Pi via GPIO

Next, we are going to experiment with using the GPIO pins again. Here, we can communicate with the Arduino much like we did with our other electronic components in earlier chapters.

We are going to build a circuit that allows the two devices to communicate over serials once more, but via their GPIO pins rather than USB. Make sure you power down the Raspberry Pi and Arduino when connecting up the electronic components.

For this, we need two resistors. This is due to the fact that the Arduino and Raspberry Pi operate at different voltages. These values are 3.3V for the Raspberry Pi and 5 volts for the Arduino. These two resistors create what is known as a **voltage divider**, which reduces the voltage of one device's output, to make it compatible with another device.

You can read more about voltage dividers, the voltage divider equation, and also find a handy calculator at the sparkfun.com website: `https://learn.sparkfun.com/tutorials/voltage-dividers`.

The resistors we need are 1.69 kOhm and a 3.3 kOhm. If you plug these values into the calculator (you can round up the 1.69 to 1.7) on the preceding website, you will get a result of 3.30V.

We now need to hook up these resistors up via the breadboard to create a circuit between the two boards.

Connect up the devices so they look as follows:

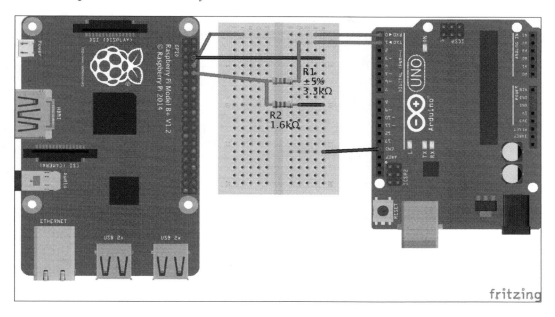

Here, we have attached a wire from Rx 0 on the Arduino to the breadboard. We then connect another wire to where we hooked up Rx 0 on the breadboard to Tx 8 on the Raspberry Pi.

Remember to cross-reference with the pin layout cheat sheet at http://pinout.xyz/ to avoid damaging your Raspberry Pi.

Following this we connect up the Tx 1 pin on the Arduino to the breadboard. A second wire is then used to connect Tx 1 via the breadboard to the leg of the 3.3 kOhm resistor. From the other leg of this resistor we then connect a wire to the Rx 10 pin on the Raspberry Pi.

Our next task is to hook up a wire from the leg of the 3.3 kOhm resistor we attached to the Raspberry Pi's pin 10 to the leg of the 1.6 kOhm resistor. After this, attach a wire from the free leg of this resistor to the ground on your breadboard, and then connect the ground of your breadboard to the GRD pin on the Arduino.

Our final task is to simply attach a wire from the Raspberry Pi's ground pin to the same ground on the breadboard as the 1.6 kOhm resistor was attached to.

We now have a working circuit for sending data between serial pins on both our devices. Let's get started on the code that will make them talk.

Start by powering up both devices again and open up the Arduino IDE.

Add this code to the new sketch:

```
void setup(){
  Serial.begin(9600);
}

void loop(){
  if (Serial.available()) {
    int num = Serial.read();
    Serial.print("Incoming data: ");
    Serial.println(num, DEC);

  }
}
```

This program is fairly similar to the previous application.

We start by setting our data transfer rate to 9600 bits per second.

Next, in the loop of the application, we check if Serial is available and then catch any sent data using the Serial.read() function. This is then stored in the num variable.

The next two lines of code output a message and the value is sent to the Arduino.

And that's it, a simple program for receiving data on the Arduino and then sending it back.

Upload this to the Arduino Uno and save the sketch as arduino_sketch_2.

Next we will write a Python program that sends the letter P to the Arduino sketch. Create a new Python program called ninth_python_prog.py and add to it the following code:

```
#!/usr/bin/python

import serial

def main():
```

```
ser_con = serial.Serial('/dev/ttyAMA0', 9600, timeout=1)
ser_con.open()

ser_con.write('1')
try:
    while 1:
        resp = ser_con.readline()
        if len(resp) > 0:
            print "The Arduino said … "
            print resp
except KeyboardInterrupt:
    ser_con.close()

if __name__ =='__main__':
    main()
```

Let's break down this code and see what the script is doing.

First we use the `import` statement to import the serial library.

Following this is our `main()` function where the action happens.

We then set up a serial connection with a data transfer rate of `9600`, as with the Arduino:

```
ser_con = serial.Serial('/dev/ttyAMA0', 9600, timeout=1)
ser_con.open()
```

Once we have defined the serial connection, we then open it.

Following this we then send the number `1` over the serial:

```
ser_con.write('1')
```

Next is the `try`/`except` statement:

```
try:
    while 1:
        if len(resp) > 0:
            print "The Arduino said … "
            print resp
except KeyboardInterrupt:
    ser_con.close()
```

Here we have a `while` loop that attempts to take a response after the number was sent. If a response is found, it is output to the screen.

The `except` statement allows us to close the script with *Ctrl* + *C* on the command line. When this happens, the serial connection is closed.

Save the file and exit. Now start it up from the command line using Python:

```
python ninth_python_prog.py
```

You should now see the two scripts transferring data to one another:

```
andydennis — pi@raspberrypi: ~/python_programs — ssh — 80×24
pi@raspberrypi ~/python_programs $ python ninth_python_prog.py
The Arduino said ...
Incoming data: 49

```

When the Python script sends the number 1 to the Arduino, it converts it into its ASCII value and then sends it back with the message `Incoming data`.

You can escape from the script using the keyboard command as we noted previously. Since the `while` loop is running infinitely, you could expand the script to start sending data constantly back and forth.

Our next experiment in communication between devices is going to use I2C.

Communication over I2C

We covered I2C in an earlier chapter and also enabled it for future use. Now we can see how to use it to communicate between the Arduino and Raspberry Pi. At this point you may want to plug your Arduino into mains power using the device's power socket.

We will be using the Raspberry Pi as the master device and the Uno as the slave. What this means will become apparent shortly. There are two important terms we also need to understand, SCL and SDA. SCL is a clock line used to synchronize data sent across the I2C bus. SDA is the data line where data is sent across.

When sending data, if we want to send a high logic signal, we send 0 volts and a low logic signal sends the device's voltage, which, in the case of the Raspberry Pi, is 3.3 volts.

Let's start by wiring up our Arduino and Raspberry Pi 2 using the I2C pins. If your devices are currently powered up, disconnect them and remove any other components attached to the GPIO pins.

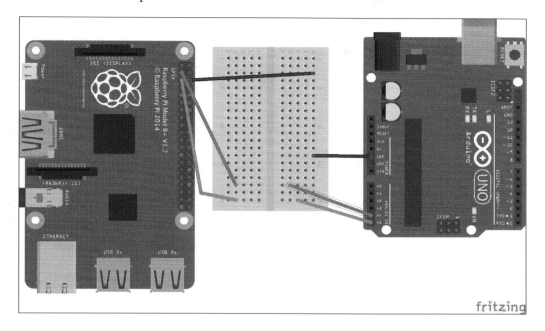

Here the GND pins are wired together via the breadboard. Next, the Uno Analog 5 pin is wired to the Raspberry Pi GPIO 0 (SDA or BCM2) and the Uno Analogue 4 to the Raspberry Pi GPIO 1 pin (SCL or BCM3).

And that's it; we are ready to explore the software side.

We now need to create a new Arduino sketch. Add the following code to this sketch:

```
#include <Wire.h>

#define SLAVE_ADDRESS 0x04

int num = 0;
int store = 0;

void setup() {

  Serial.begin(9600);
  Wire.begin(SLAVE_ADDRESS);
  Wire.onReceive(recData);
  Wire.onRequest(sendData);
```

```
  }

  void loop() {
    delay(100);
  }

  void sendData(){
    Wire.write(num);
  }

  void recData(int byteCount){

    while(Wire.available()) {
      store = Wire.read();
      Serial.print("Data received: ");
      Serial.println(store);
    }

  }
```

We will now walk through what this sketch does.

First of all, we import the `Wire` library into our sketch. This is used for I2C communication. You can read more about the library at the Arduino website: `https://www.arduino.cc/en/Reference/Wire`.

Following this, we define the `SLAVE_ADDRESS`. This defines the byte address we will use to communicate between our two devices.

The terms *master* and *slave* are used when implementing I2C. Master devices drive the SCL clock line and slave devices respond to the master. Our Arduino will be the slave device. This is because the Raspberry Pi header has a built in resistor where the pin is located and thus when we send a high logic signal, we send 3.3 volts to the Arduino.

The Arduino registers the 3.3 volts as a low signal; therefore, by sending 0 or 3.3 volts we can switch between high and low logic values when communicating between the Raspberry Pi and Arduino.

You can read more about the master and slave method at the following website: `http://www.robot-electronics.co.uk/i2c-tutorial`.

The next line of code defines a global variable called `num`, which stores the value `0`. This value is used later in our sketch in one of the functions, which we will explore shortly. The following `store` variable is used to capture the data sent from the Raspberry Pi.

After this is the `setup` function:

```
Serial.begin(9600);
Wire.begin(SLAVE_ADDRESS);
Wire.onReceive(recData);
Wire.onRequest(sendData);
```

Here, we initialize the serial connection with a baud rate of `9600`.

The next line initializes the Arduino as the slave device using the value we stored in the `SLAVE_ADDRESS` variable.

Following this, we define that when we receive data or send data we reference a callback function. This means we pass in a function as a parameter to the `onReceive` and `onRequest` functions. These two functions, `recData()` and `sendData()`, are defined later in the sketch.

Next in the sketch is the loop function. This contains a single line of code:

```
delay(100);
```

Here we can see we add a slight pause each time the loop is executed.

Our next function definition is as follows:

```
void sendData(){
  Wire.write(num);
}
```

The `sendData()` function simply sends the value of the `num` variable, that is, `0`.

Its counterpart callback function is `recData()`.

```
void recData(int byteCount){

  while(Wire.available()) {
    store = Wire.read();
    Serial.print("Data received: ");
    Serial.println(store);
  }

}
```

Inside this function definition is a `while` loop. Until the I2C connection is lost, the loop will continuously execute. The loop contains code that stores incoming data in the `store` variable.

We then take this result and print out a message and its value to the serial console.

Save this file as `arduino_sketch_three` and upload it to the Arduino.

This concludes the Arduino sketch. Let's now take a look at its Python counterpart.

Create a new file in the `python_programs` directory called `tenth_python_prog.py`.

To this file add the following code:

```python
#!/usr/bin/python

import smbus
import time

bus = smbus.SMBus(1)
addr = 0x04

def main():
    while True:
        sendNum(1)
        time.sleep(1)
        num = readNum()
        print "The num is", num

def sendNum(value):
    bus.write_byte(addr, value)
    return -1

def readNum():
    num = bus.read_byte(addr)
    return num

if __name__ == '__main__':
    main()
```

This Python script accepts an input and sends a value back to the Arduino. In this case it will receive a 0 from the Arduino and then send the value 1 back to it.

We start the sketch by importing the necessary libraries. The smbus library is used to handle our I2C calls.

Following this is the `time` library, which we can use to pause the script using the `sleep` function.

We then define two variables:

```
bus = smbus.SMBus(1)
addr = 0x04
```

The `bus` variable stores the value of the connection to the I2C bus. Following this, we store the value of the address. This is the same value as we used in the Arduino sketch.

After the variable definition is the `main()` function definition. Inside this is a `while` loop:

```
while True:
    sendNum(1)
    time.sleep(1)
    num = readNum()
    print "The num is", num
```

The `while` loop continues infinitely and performs the following tasks:

- Send the number 1 to the Arduino
- Pause momentarily
- Receive the value sent by the Arduino and store it in the `num` variable
- Print out a message with the value of `num`

The next function to be defined is `sendNum()`:

```
def sendNum(value):
    bus.write_byte(address, value)
    return -1
```

Here, we write the integer value to the byte address and then exit the function.

Its counterpart is the function that receives data:

```
def readNum():
    num = bus.read_byte(addr)
    return num
```

The `readNum()` function listens for data being sent from the defined address and then returns it.

Finally, we wrap up the script with a call to the `main` function.

Save this file and exit the text editor. We can now test the two scripts.

The Arduino sketch should be running. Start up the Python script from the command line:

```
python tenth_python_prog.py
```

You will now see the scripts sending data to each other. On the Raspberry Pi command line you should see this output:

```
The num is 0
The num is 0
```

And you should see this output on the Arduino serial monitor:

```
Data received: 1
```

A nice addition to the script would be to add the code to catch the keyboard interrupt so we exit the script gracefully. You could also include a `try catch` loop for capturing any other exceptions that are thrown. This concludes our experiment with I2C.

We will now look at one final example before concluding this chapter.

Communication over the Web

Finally, we can use HTTP to send data between our two devices. If you purchased an Arduino Ethernet shield, attach this to the Uno now and connect it to your home network via an Ethernet cable.

The Arduino comes with example code for setting up a small web server, which can leverage the Ethernet shield.

Open the **Examples** menu from **File** | **Examples** | **Ethernet** | **Web Server**.

Depending on your home network, you will need to modify this line of code to use a free IP address:

```
IPAddress ip(192, 168, 1, 177);
```

Once this is updated upload the sketch to the Arduino.

The sketch performs the simple task of checking the values on the analog pins and then printing this to anyone who connects to the Uno over HTTP.

If you don't attach any electronics to the analog pins then you should expect to see no results. This project can be expanded to incorporate a number of electronic devices that read/write data back to the analog pins.

On your Raspberry Pi, enter the IP address of the Arduino into a browser and connect to the address. You should now see a webpage displayed.

Using the information from earlier chapters, you can now modify the HTML code to display more details to the visitor.

This concludes our simple example of HTTP communication between the two devices. A number of other examples, which are interesting to experiment with, can be found in the Arduino IDE.

Summary

This concludes our chapter on working with the Raspberry Pi 2 and the Arduino microcontroller.

Here, we learned how we could communicate over USB, GPIO, and I2C. This brought together some of the tasks we performed in earlier chapters.

Next is the final chapter of the book! Here we will build a project that uses some of the skills you have learned so far. You'll test your experience of working with GPIO pins, the Python programming language, and web development. Finally, you'll be presented with some ideas on how to expand your project further.

So let's get started.

11
Final Project

Over the course of this book you have studied a number of subjects, including:

- The Python programming language
- C and C++
- SQLite
- Assembler
- Graphics programming
- Audio programming
- GPIO pins
- Interacting with electronics
- Integrating third-party microcontrollers

We are now going to build a project that brings many of these ideas together. In this chapter, we are going to construct an inventory management device. This will use a combination of SQLite, Python, the GPIO pins, a web server, and an LED.

Our project will store information about items stored in our kitchen. It will then allow us to update this inventory through a web interface. When an item gets low, for example when fewer than two are left, it will trigger an LED to switch on.

Once we have our basic software and electronics in place, some ideas for extending the project further will be presented.

Let's start by getting our Raspberry Pi hardware set up.

Choose your storage mechanism

We recommend you store the website and inventory management system on the external hard drive. Of course, if you wish to skip this step, you can, and can simply use the SD card. However, this will give you the chance to experiment with the information provided in *Chapter 5, Expanding on Storage Options*.

We are now going to create a sub-directory called `final_project` to store our source code and database. This will either be on the external HD or on the microSD card, depending on what you choose as your storage mechanism. All of our development work will have in this directory.

Once this is done, navigate into it and you will be ready to start building the website.

Building a Flask-based website

You will be familiar with the basics of Flask from *Chapter 9, Building a Web Server*. Once again, we will be using this framework to create a website that can interact with a database.

You can always refer to the Flask documentation site if you find a feature you wish to learn more about: `http://flask.pocoo.org/docs/0.10/`

Our project will involve creating a number of web forms that can update our SQLite database with information on what items are stocked in our inventory.

First, we need to create a database to store our inventory data in.

Adding a database

In our previous SQL example, we logged in to SQLite to create the database. We can in fact write our SQL in a separate file and dump this into SQLite. This makes managing our source code a lot easier, and we can also re-run it against an empty database whenever we wish.

So we will therefore take our existing data model from *Chapter 9, Building a Web Server* and convert it into an SQL file. We will also include the INSERT INTO statements along with a collection of items.

Create a new empty file called `inventory_schema.sql`.

To this, add the following code:

```
/* Create tables/Data Model */
```

```
CREATE TABLE storage_location (id INTEGER PRIMARY KEY AUTOINCREMENT,
location VARCHAR(25));
```

```
CREATE TABLE food_item (id INTEGER PRIMARY KEY AUTOINCREMENT, description
VARCHAR(40), location INTEGER, FOREIGN KEY(location) REFERENCES storage_
location(id));
```

```
/*Insert data*/
```

```
INSERT INTO storage_location (location) VALUES ('Fridge'),('Cupboard'),('
Draw');
```

```
INSERT INTO food_item (location, description) VALUES (1, 'Eggs'),
```

```
(1, 'Sausages'),(1, 'Steaks'),(2, 'Pasta sauce'),(2, 'Canned peas'),
```

```
(2, 'Canned beans'),(3, 'Spaghetti');
```

This is simply an expansion of the DB we built before. Save the file. We can create a new database using this file with the following command:

```
sqlite3 inventory.db < inventory_schema.sql
```

Once this command runs, open up the database in SQLite.

Try running `SELECT * FROM food_item;` and you will see the food you imported via the SQL file.

Now we have a database in place, we can build an app to sit over it.

A basic website

Our next task is going to be to write the Python and HTML code needed for the inventory management system.

We are going to create two further directories called `static` and `templates` to store our website code in.

Once this is done, create a new Python file called `inventory.py` and open it in your text editor.

This file will contain our applications code. To this file, add in the following:

```
#!/usr/bin/python

from flask import Flask,request, session, g, redirect, url_for, abort,
render_template, flash
```

```
import sqlite3

DATABASE = 'inventory.db'
SECRET_KEY = '1234'

app = Flask(__name__)
app.config.from_object(__name__)


def db_connection():
    return sqlite3.connect(app.config['DATABASE'])

@app.before_request
def before_request():
    g.db = db_connection()

@app.teardown_request
def teardown_request(exception):
    db = getattr(g, 'db', None)
    if db is not None:
        db.close()

@app.route('/')
def show_inventory():
    cur = g.db.execute("SELECT food_item.description, storage_
location.location FROM food_item INNER JOIN storage_location ON food_
item.location WHERE storage_location.id==food_item.location;")
    inventory = [dict(description=row[0], location=row[1]) for row in
cur.fetchall()]
    return render_template('display_inventory.html',
inventory=inventory)

if __name__ == '__main__':
    app.run(debug=True, host='0.0.0.0')
```

You will be familiar with the concepts displayed in a lot of this code from your earlier website project. However, we have included a number of new features. Let's take a look at these.

The first are some settings used by the application, these being:

```
DATABASE = 'inventory.db'
SECRET_KEY = '1234'
```

The DATABASE value contains our inventory SQLite DB. The next setting is the SECRET_KEY, which is needed when implementing sessions in a Flask application.

Following this, we include three functions for handling the database functions, these being:

```
def db_connection():
    return sqlite3.connect(app.config['DATABASE'])

@app.before_request
def before_request():
    g.db = db_connection()

@app.teardown_request
def teardown_request(exception):
    db = getattr(g, 'db', None)
    if db is not None:
        db.close()
```

The methods are responsible for opening a DB connection, and closing the connection when we are finished with it.

The final portion of this code that is new is located within the show_inventory() function.

As you can see, we have included a query to return all the items in the inventory database and have included code that passes the results to our template as a variable. This can be seen in the following block of code:

```
return render_template('display_inventory.html', inventory=inventory)
```

Of course, this now leads us to the next item we need to setup—a template to display these results. This will be written in HTML, which you should be familiar with from our first web application.

Navigate into the templates directory and create a new file called template.html. To this file, add the following:

```
<!doctype html>
<title>Inventory management system</title>
<link rel=stylesheet type=text/css href="{{ url_for('static',
filename='style.css') }}">
<div class=page>
  <h1>Inventory management system</h1>
  {% block body %}{% endblock %}
</div>
```

This code will form the base template that all of our web forms will inherit from. It uses a technology called Jinja, which provides a template mechanism for Python projects. When we implement Jinja web templates, we can pass variables from our Python code to the template and display the results in HTML.

You can read more about Jinja here: http://jinja.pocoo.org/docs/dev/.

In this block of HTML code, we can see where Jinja has been implemented. This includes:

```
href="{{ url_for('static', filename='style.css') }}"
```

It also includes:

```
{% block body %}{% endblock %}
```

Our piece of code is used to include a CSS file from the static directory we created. The second is used to provide an area where our page templates will be rendered. You'll see how this works in more detail next.

We now need to create the HTML that will render the inventory contents on the screen. Create a file under the `templates` directory called `display_inventory.html`.

To this file, add the following:

```
{% extends "template.html" %}
{% block body %}
  <ul class="items">
  {% for item in inventory %}
    <li><h2>{{ item.description }}</h2>{{ item.location }}
  {% else %}
    <li><em>Your inventory is empty</em>
  {% endfor %}
  </ul>
{% endblock %}
```

This code renders the results from the query we constructed in our application code. You can see in the `for` loop that the `inventory` variable is iterated through and its results are embedded in the HTML code. If the inventory is empty, then we display a message to the user.

This code is rendered inside the `body` block we created within the `template.html` file. We achieve this through including the `extends` keyword with the name of the base template. Next, we wrap the code we want rendered in the name of the block from the base template where it will be displayed, in this case `body`. Save this file and exit.

Let's try checking what we have developed so far. From the command line, run:

```
python inventory.py
```

Once the app is running, navigate to the URL and port where your site will be displayed. You should now see a list of items and their location.

So you may notice we are missing a count. Wouldn't be nice if we knew how many of each of these items we had? Stop the application and let's add this feature.

We can open the existing SQLite database and run the following command to add a column to the `food_item` table that contains a count of the number of items:

```
ALTER TABLE food_item ADD COLUMN num INTEGER;
```

If you like, go back and edit your existing `inventory_schema.sql` file to include this column. Then next time you create a new database from scratch, it will be included.

With a column to store the value, we can now update our `Eggs` so there are three of them. To do this, run the following command:

```
UPDATE food_item SET num = 3 WHERE id = 1;
```

Once again, you can modify your existing SQL file to include counts for each of the items you insert.

We can now exit SQLite shell and update the HTML and Python code to show the count on the web page. First we will edit the HTML template, `display_inventory.html`:

```
<li><h2>{{ item.description }}</h2>{{ item.location }},{{item.count}}
```

Here, we have added in {{item.count}}, which will display the number of items that exist.

Next, we can update the Python code to include the count of items and pass it to the HTML template. To the query embedded in the Python code, add the following:

```
food_item.num
```

Next, update the variable `inventory` to return it to the HTML page:

```
inventory = [dict(description=row[0], location=row[1], count=row[2])
for row in cur.fetchall()]
```

You can save this file and restart the application.

Now check the web page again you should see the count!

 Remember you can use the SELECT statement to get the ID of the column you are updating.

Let's now include the functionality to add and edit items in our inventory.

Web forms

Web forms are the mechanism by which we add, edit, and delete data from the database. They provide an easy method for a user to update values via their web browser.

We will need two forms, these being the add form and edit form. The edit form will also double up as the delete form, allowing us to update existing items in an inventory.

Let's start by creating the add functionality.

Add

You will need to start by creating some code to handle the addition of a new item via Python. Open up the inventory.py file and add in the following functions above if __name__: == '__main__':

```
@app.route('/add_item')
def add_item():
    return render_template('add_item.html')


@app.route('/add', methods=['POST'])
def add_to_db():
    g.db.execute('INSERT INTO food_item (description, location, num)
VALUES (?, ?, ?)',
                 [request.form['description'], request.
form['location'], request.form['num']])
    g.db.commit()
    flash('New inventory item added')
    return redirect(url_for('show_inventory'))
```

Here we have added in the add_item() function, which routes traffic to the HTML form add_item.html that we will create shortly.

Next, we include a function to insert values passed by the web form POST method into the database. Once this has been committed, we flash a message to the user and redirect them back to the `display_inventory.html` page, where they can see their new item.

Let's now create the `add_item.html` page in the `templates` directory. To this file, add the following:

```
{% extends "template.html" %}
{% block body %}
    <form action="{{ url_for('add_to_db') }}" method=POST class="add-
item">
        <div>Description: <input type="text" size="30"
name="description"></div>
        <div>Location: <input type="text" size="30" name="location"></
div>
        <div>Number of items to add: <input type="text" size="30"
name="num"></div>
        <div><input type="submit" value="Add item"></div>
    </form>
{% endblock %}
```

This is a simple web form embedded in the `body` block.

The `action` value is set to point to the `add_to_db()` method we just created. When we submit the form, it will POST the values back to our Flask application, which can then add the values to the database.

Save this file and start up the inventory application again. To test the new form that was created, access it via the following URL: `http://<rpi ip address>/add_item`

From here, you can now add a new item. When you submit the form, you will then be redirected to the inventory page and see the new item there.

You may notice some problems with this form, however. First, we have to enter a number for the location. It would be better if this had a dropdown list of existing locations.

Also, what if an item already exists; do we want to add it again? What if it is in more than one location?

Let's first modify the `add_item()` function so we pull a list of locations back in their descriptive form. Stop the application and open up `inventory.py`. Edit the function so it looks as follows:

```
@app.route('/add_item')
def add_item():
    cur = g.db.execute("SELECT id, location FROM storage_location;")
```

```
        location = [dict(id=row[0], location=row[1]) for row in cur.
fetchall()]
        return render_template('add_item.html', location=location)
```

Here, we have added in a query that pulls back the descriptive name of each location and passes it to the `add_item.html` template as a variable. With this value now available to be displayed, we can edit the form to include it.

We'll be using a dropdown list to display these values. Modify your code to replace the location with the following:

```
<select name="location">
  {% for place in location %}
    <option value={{place.id}}>{{place.location}}</option>
  {% endfor %}
</select>
```

Using the Jinja `for` loop, we have built up the values in a dropdown list and included the ID of each of the locations. When we submit the form, we pass the ID back rather than the descriptive version of the location so we can insert the new record.

Save the form and restart the application. When you try adding a new value to the database, you should now see the dropdown list present.

We are still left with the problem of deciding whether we can add an existing item to a new location or allow duplicates of an item.

One way around this is to have a table that links items to locations and the number of each item stored at that location.

See if you can work out how to implement this change!

Since we can add new items, we'll need to be able to edit them to update the count. Let's look at this next.

Edit

We will now update the inventory application to present a web form that allows us to add and remove the number of each item we have in the inventory.

To the `inventory.py` file, add the following code:

```
@app.route('/edit_item')
def edit_item():
    cur = g.db.execute("SELECT food_item.id, food_item.description,
food_item.location, food_item.num FROM food_item INNER JOIN storage_
location ON food_item.location WHERE storage_location.id==food_item.
location;")
```

```
    items = [dict(id=row[0], description=row[1], location=row[2],
num=row[3]) for row in cur.fetchall()]
    return render_template('edit_items.html', items=items)


@app.route('/edit', methods=['POST'])
def edit_in_db():
    g.db.execute('UPDATE food_item SET num = ? WHERE id = ?',
                  [request.form['num'], request.form['id']])
    g.db.commit()
    flash('Item updated')
    return redirect(url_for('edit_item'))
```

These two methods are not dissimilar to those that we used to add items to the database. Our first function, `edit_item()`, returns a list of items from the database along with their location and count, and passes the results to a template.

The second function handles an incoming POST request and updates the count for the relevant item we are editing.

Save this file and create a new HTML template under `templates` called `edit_items.html`. To this file, add the following code:

```
{% extends "template.html" %}
{% block body %}
  {% for item in items %}
    <form action="{{ url_for('edit_in_db') }}" method=POST
class="edit-item">
    <div>
    <input type="hidden" name="id" value={{item.id}}>
    <h2>{{item.description}}</h2>
    Storage location: {{item.location}}<br />
    Update number of items: <input name="num" type="text"
value={{item.num}}>
    </div>
       <div><input type="submit" value="Edit item"></div>
    </form>
  {% endfor %}
{% endblock %}
```

This template is very similar to the one we used to add items. Here though we have included a hidden input field. This is used to store the ID of the item we are editing. When we submit the form back to the application, it will use this ID in the query that updates the item count.

Save this file and restart your application. You should now be able to edit an existing item.

Do you see that the location is still a number? Think about how you could modify the query to return the description rather than the ID.

Finally, you may remember we added a static directory. This can be used to store a CSS file for styling your web pages. In this directory, create a new file called style.css.

Throughout the HTML templates we created, you will see a number of CSS classes specified. You can try adding your own styling for these class names to the style. css file. When the web page renders, it will include your styling.

For a guide to styling, you can review the following CSS information: http://www. w3schools.com/css/.

So we have our web application up and running. Let's look at how we can use it to interact with some other hardware. Next we are going to add an LED, which lights up when we get low on items in our inventory.

Adding in an LED

You'll already be familiar with how to control an LED from *Chapter 7, Exploring the Raspberry Pi's GPIO Pins*. In this instance, we will once again hook the LED up to the Raspberry Pi's GPIO pins. We will then switch it on and off based upon whether one of the categories of items in our inventory has fewer than two items left.

Building the circuit – a recap

We will quickly recap on setting up the circuit for the LED. The following diagram demonstrates this again:

Here, we have connected an LED to a 270 Ohm resistor and hooked this up to GPIO pin 4. Finally, the LED's other leg is connected to the ground pin.

This circuit is now ready to be controlled from our Flask application.

Integrating with our Python app

Now we have the circuit up and running again, we can hook it into our existing Python functions and have them switch the LED on and off.

What we will need to do is trigger the LED to switch on when we edit an item if the count is now less than 2, that is, there are 0 or 1 items left.

Open up the inventory.py file.

To the top of the file, we need to add a new import statement:

```
import RPi.GPIO as GPIO
```

This includes the RPi.GPIO library, which you'll remember from our previous project.

After this, we need to set up the LED to say it is connected to GPIO pin 4. Add this code in the following settings for the DATABASE and SECRET_KEY:

```
LED = 4
```

Now we can update our before_request function to include support for GPIO. Modify the function to include the code for setting up the GPIO pin:

```
@app.before_request
def before_request():
    GPIO.setmode(GPIO.BCM)
    GPIO.setwarnings(False)
    GPIO.setup(LED, GPIO.OUT)
    g.db = db_connection()
```

After this, update the teardown_request method to call the cleanup function:

```
@app.teardown_request
def teardown_request(exception):
    GPIO.cleanup()
    db = getattr(g, 'db', None)
    if db is not None:
        db.close()
```

Next, we need to switch the LED on when we have fewer than two items. We do this by updating the `edit_item()` function with the following `if else` statement:

```
@app.route('/edit_item')
def edit_item():
    led_on = False
    cur = g.db.execute("SELECT food_item.id, food_item.description,
food_item.location, food_item.num FROM food_item INNER JOIN storage_
location ON food_item.location WHERE storage_location.id==food_item.
location;")
    items = [dict(id=row[0], description=row[1], location=row[2],
num=row[3]) for row in cur.fetchall()]
    for i in items:
        if i['num'] < 2:
            led_on = True
    if led_on:
        GPIO.output(LED, 1)
    else:
        GPIO.output(LED, 0)

    return render_template('edit_items.html', items=items)
```

Every time we edit the inventory, we run a check to see if any of the items have fewer than two left. If this is the case, then the LED is switched on. If not, then the LED is switched off.

As you can see, this is a fairly simple change to our inventory management system, but opens up lots of possibilities for expanding our circuit to perform other tasks.

Save the file and let's test out the change.

Start up the inventory application again with `sudo` and navigate to the edit form.

Edit one of your items and submit the change. You should see the LED switches on. This is because when we initially added items to the database, we didn't add a count to many of the items. If you happened to add a count to each of the items when testing the edit form before, then the LED should be off.

Edit each of the items so that they have a count greater than 2. You will see the LED switches off.

Now try changing the value associated with the number of `Eggs` you have to `1`. On submitting the form, the LED will switch on again.

We now have a basic inventory management system. It can be updated via web forms and stores data in the database. When we have fewer than two of any item, then an LED is switched on.

Congratulations, you have completed the concluding chapter in this book's project.

So how can we extend this further?

Extending the project further

Now you have a working system, you can consider adding more functionality to it. We provide you with some ideas in the following sections with links that will help you to implement the functionality.

Replace the LED with a screen

While an LED is a neat feature, it would be nice to know which item has only one left in the inventory. The LED also does not distinguish between multiple items being in short supply. In fact, we have to check via the web browser to see what items are stocked.

One way around this is to integrate a screen with the Raspberry Pi. You could place the Raspberry Pi in your kitchen and check the screen to see what is in short supply.

Thankfully this is an easy task. The Raspberry Pi Foundation released a digital touch screen you can connect to your Raspberry Pi's GPIO pins.

You can read more about it here: `https://www.raspberrypi.org/products/raspberry-pi-touch-display/`.

In addition, hooking up a screen like this will allow you to experiment with the skills you learned in *Chapter 6, Low-Level Graphics Programming*.

E-mail support

A useful feature could be to receive an e-mail when somebody uses the last of an item. For example, you could be at work and somebody uses the last egg in the fridge. This would then trigger an e-mail reminding you to pick up some more on the way home.

Implementing e-mails via Python is very simple. The following guide on the Python website shows how you can expand a program to support this functionality: `https://docs.python.org/2/library/email-examples.html`.

You could, for example, update the `edit_item()` function to include the e-mail triggering functionality.

If you choose to add e-mail support, an existing e-mail account on a service such as Gmail can be used.

The following website provides an example of how to configure this: `http://www.pythonforbeginners.com/google/sending-emails-using-google`.

Playing a sound

We already looked at the sound capabilities of the Raspberry Pi. Perhaps we could implement some functionality so when we run out of an item a sound plays?

There are a number of ways of doing this, including via Python. As you will remember from *Chapter 8, Exploring Sound with the Raspberry Pi 2*, we can play sounds via the `os.system` command, such as:

```
os.system('mpg123 -q drum2.mp3 &')
```

Expanding your code base to include this would be very simple and could trigger an MP3 when the LED is switched on.

Summary

In this chapter we built an inventory management system that was a combination of hardware and software. We further explored some of the Raspberry Pi's features that were covered throughout the book.

Finally, we provided you with a list of ideas to extend the project further and implement new features. This concludes the book and now its over to you the reader to explore further.

Index

Symbols

.balign directive
  about 54
  reference link 54
.data directive
  .balign directive 54
  about 53
  labels 54
  word 54

A

Acorn RISC Machine (ARM)
  about 46
  reference link 48, 60
addresses 52, 55
Amixer
  reference link 135
Apache
  about 156
  reference link 156, 158
application
  compiling 38, 110
  running 38, 110
apt-get
  about 19
  reference link 19
Arduino
  and Raspberry Pi communication,
      via GPIO 178-182
  communication, over I2C 182-188
  communication, over Web 188, 189

integrating with 175
  reference link 172
  serial communication, over USB 175-178
  website link 172-184
Arduino IDE 174
Arduino shields
  reference link 122
Arduino software
  reference link 173
  setting up 173
ARM instruction set
  reference link 50
assembler 49
assembly language 26-28
audio interactions, through GPIO
  about 136
  audio drivers, installing 136
  audio shields, for Raspberry Pi 142
  drivers, loading 137, 138
  drum tracks, obtaining 138
  hardware setup 136, 137
  Python drum machine 138141
  reference link 142
audio output, Raspberry Pi
  reference link 5
audio setup
  reference link 135
available web servers
  about 156
  Apache 156, 157
  NGINX 158, 159

B

F

favicon
  adding, to Python web server 162
  reference link 162
fb.h library
  reference link 98
fibers 65
file
  Python program, running from 42, 43
File Allocation Table (FAT)
  about 10
  reference link 10
Flask
  about 166-168
  reference link 166, 168
Flask-based website
  building 192
  database, adding 192, 193
for loop
  reference link 61
frame buffer
  accessing 96, 97
  C code, testing 100
  display settings, checking 97-99

G

GCC compiler
  reference link 37, 50
g++ command 76
Geany
  about 33
  reference link 34
general purpose input/output. *See* GPIO
Genuino/Arduino microcontroller
  reference link 173
Git
  reference link 124
GPIO
  about 113
  audio interactions 135
  power voltages 120

GPIO pins
  about 5, 113
  data, reading 129
  direct connection 123
  I2C 115, 116
  power voltages 120
  PPM 119
  Pulse Position Modulation (PPM) 119
  Pulse Width Modulation (PWM) 119
  reference link 114, 120
  Rx 117
  Serial Peripheral Interface (SPI) 118
  standard GPIO 114
  testing 23
  Tx 117

H

hardware options
  about 120
  boards, prototyping 120, 121
  Cooking Hacks Arduino bridge
     shield 121, 122
  shields, prototyping 120, 121
hardware specifications, Raspberry Pi 2
HiFiBerri
  reference link 142
Humble Pi
  reference link 121
hybrid threads
  reference links 66
Hyper Text Markup Language (HTML)
  about 155
  document styling, reference link 156
  reference link 156, 162
Hypertext Transfer Protocol (HTTP)
  about 154
  reference link 154

I

I2C
  about 115, 116
  in Python applications, reference link 115
  real time clock, reference link 117